MOONBIRD

A YEAR ON THE WIND
WITH THE GREAT SURVIVOR B95

MOONBIRD

A YEAR ON THE WIND
WITH THE GREAT SURVIVOR B95

PHILLIP HOOSE

FARRAR STRAUS GIROUX

New York

Farrar Straus Giroux Books for Young Readers
175 Fifth Avenue, New York 10010

Text copyright © 2012 by Phillip Hoose
Maps copyright © 2012 by Jeffrey L. Ward
All rights reserved
Distributed in Canada by D&M Publishers, Inc.
Printed in China by Toppan Leefung Printing Ltd.,
Dongguan City, Guangdong Province
Designed by Roberta Pressel
First edition, 2012
1 3 5 7 9 10 8 6 4 2

mackids.com

Library of Congress Cataloging-in-Publication Data
Hoose, Phillip M., 1947–
    Moonbird : a year on the wind with the great survivor B95 / Phillip
Hoose. — 1st ed.
        p.   cm.
    ISBN 978-0-374-30468-3
    1. Red knot—Migration—Juvenile literature.   2. Red knot—
Juvenile literature.   3. Bird watching—Juvenile literature.   I. Title.

QL696.C48H66 2012
598.072'34—dc23
                                                            2011035612

For Sandi

CONTENTS

MOONBIRD

A YEAR ON THE WIND
WITH THE GREAT SURVIVOR B95

MEET B95, ONE OF THE WORLD'S PREMIER ATHLETES. Weighing a mere four ounces, he's flown more than 325,000 miles in his life—the distance to the moon and nearly halfway back. He flies at mountaintop height along ancient routes that lead him to his breeding grounds and back. But changes throughout his migratory circuit are challenging this Superbird and threatening to wipe out his entire subspecies of *rufa* red knot. Places that are critical for B95 and his flock to rest and refuel—stepping-stones along a vast annual migration network—have been altered by human activity. Can these places and the food they contain be preserved?

Or will B95's and *rufa*'s days of flight soon come to an end?

INTRODUCTION

B95 CAN FEEL IT: A STIRRING IN HIS BONES AND FEATHERS. It's time. Today is the day he will once again cast himself into the air, spiral upward into the clouds, and bank into the wind, working his newly molted flight feathers for real. After weeks of flight testing he feels ready. Day by day, he has spent the nonfeeding hours during high tide carefully smoothing the barbs on each feather vane to seamless perfection. Now there are no gaps for the wind to pass through and slow him down. He has packed all the fuel he can, gorging on worms, clams, mussels, and tiny crustaceans. His inner GPS is set for north. The whole flock is rippling with anticipation, chattering, waiting for one of them to make the first move.

In the next few months, from March to June, B95 and his flock mates will fly from the bottom of the world to the top—from the land of penguins to polar bear country. He will fly night and day, descending only to visit the regular fueling stations that have sustained him with protein all his life. He will arrive at each stop ravenously hungry, weighing much less than he did just days before. But if the food is there, and he can get to it, he will survive, refuel, and fly on.

B95 is a red knot of the subspecies *rufa*, a robin-size shorebird with streamlined wings that crook at the elbow and taper to a point. In northern spring and summer, his breast and much of his face are colored brilliant brick red, with reddish feathers sprinkled over his back. During the remainder of the year, his feathers change and his body becomes mostly gray and white.

B95's name—and fame—comes from the letter-and-number combination inscribed on an orange plastic flag fastened around his upper left leg. He is a perfectly formed male with a long bill and powerful chest. Throughout the course of his extraordinarily long life—about twenty years—scientists have captured and examined him four times, and observed him through binoculars and spotting scopes on dozens of other occasions. Because he is so old, and has survived so many difficult journeys, he has become the most celebrated shorebird in the world.

But trip by trip, B95 threads the sky with fewer companions. When he was first banded as a young bird in 1995, scientists estimated there were about 150,000 *rufa* red knots in existence. Then, around the year 2000, these birds began dying by the thousands. Why? Evidence points to abrupt changes in the stopover sites along their Great Circuit, and even in the air through which they fly. A special challenge is the reduction of a very important source of food at Delaware Bay. B95's plight, and that of *rufa* red knots in general, poses one of the great conservation questions of recent years: Can humans and shorebirds coexist?

Answers will have to arrive soon, for now experts believe that fewer than 25,000 *rufa* red knots remain. That means that more than 80 percent of the population has disappeared just within B95's lifetime. This looming shadow of extinction makes B95's long life all the more improbable. Scientists ask themselves: How can this one bird keep going year after year when so many of his companions drop from the sky or perish on the beaches?

B95's gritty success inspires action. A worldwide network of scientists, conservationists, researchers, students, and volunteers has sprung up to save *rufa* from extinction. Though they are stationed around the world, they team up to follow the knots as they migrate throughout the western hemisphere, communicating instantly with new, Web-based tools. They know they have their work cut out for them, but, like B95 himself, they are determined.

As the wind ruffles his new flight feathers and the chattering flock tenses for another season's liftoff, B95 knows exactly where to go and what to do. But he doesn't know what will await him as he heads north. Will he find the banquet of horseshoe crab eggs he depends on when he arrives, starving, at Delaware Bay six weeks from now? Does a red tide outbreak like the one that killed so many birds in Uruguay await this flock? Will the skies over the Atlantic Ocean roar with tropical storms that will push him far off course? Will he ever see this Patagonian beach again?

The flock stirs, the urge to go becomes irresistible, and the knots lift as one, flashing gray and red, hundreds flying in tight formation, spiraling up into the clouds as if controlled by a single will. They take several practice circles together, and then rise and bank northward. For B95 and his companions it is another season of flight.

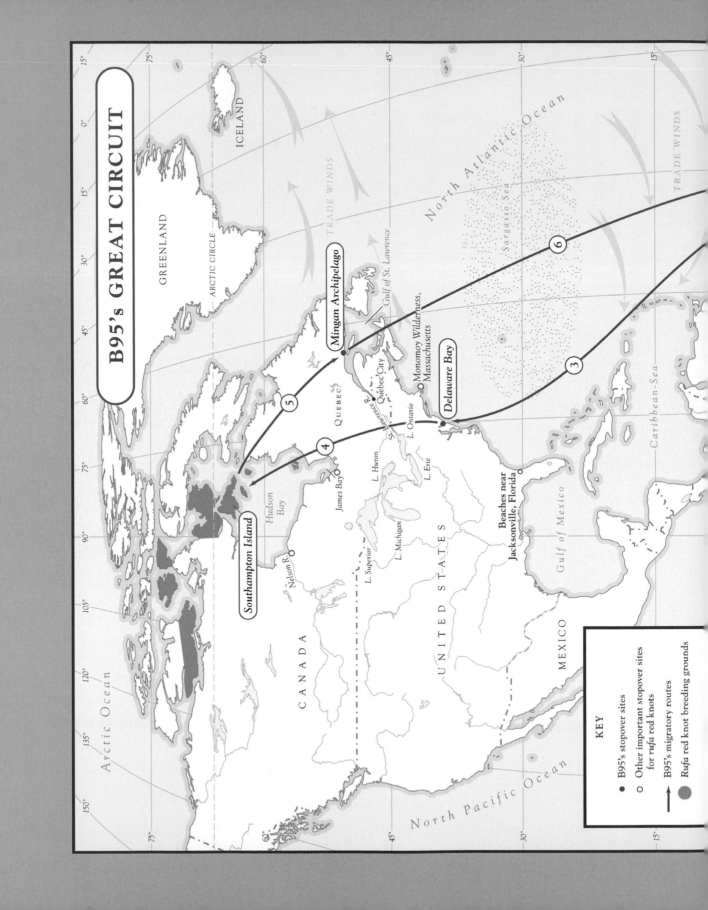

B95's GREAT CIRCUIT

KEY

- • B95's stopover sites
- ○ Other important stopover sites for *rufa* red knots
- → B95's migratory routes
- ● *Rufa* red knot breeding grounds

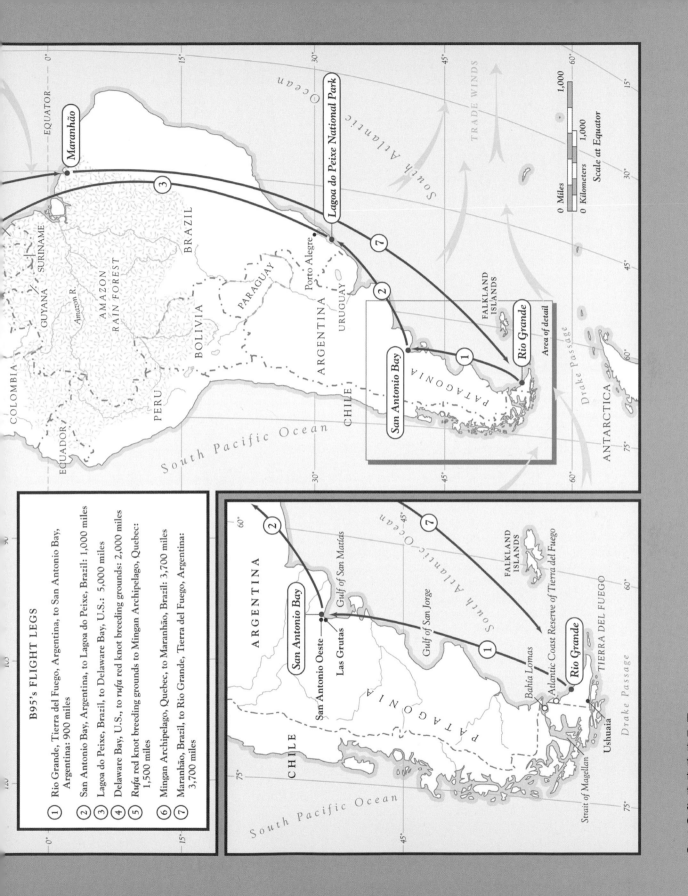

EQUATOR 0°

Maranhão

Lagoa do Peixe National Park

South Atlantic Ocean

TRADE WINDS

③

⑦

Porto Alegre

②

BRAZIL

AMAZON RAIN FOREST

Amazon R.

COLOMBIA
GUYANA
SURINAME
VENEZUELA

PARAGUAY

BOLIVIA

URUGUAY

ARGENTINA

PERU

ECUADOR

CHILE

South Pacific Ocean

FALKLAND ISLANDS

Rio Grande

Area of detail

②

①

San Antonio Bay

PATAGONIA

Drake Passage

ANTARCTICA

1,000
1,000
Scale at Equator
0 Miles
0 Kilometers

ARGENTINA

CHILE

San Antonio Bay

San Antonio Oeste

Las Grutas

Gulf of San Matías

Gulf of San Jorge

②

⑦

South Atlantic Ocean

FALKLAND ISLANDS

Bahía Lomas

Atlantic Coast Reserve of Tierra del Fuego

①

Rio Grande

TIERRA DEL FUEGO

Ushuaia

Strait of Magellan

Drake Passage

PATAGONIA

South Pacific Ocean

B95's amazing migration circuit takes him from the bottom of the earth to the top and back again, a distance of approximately 18,000 miles each year

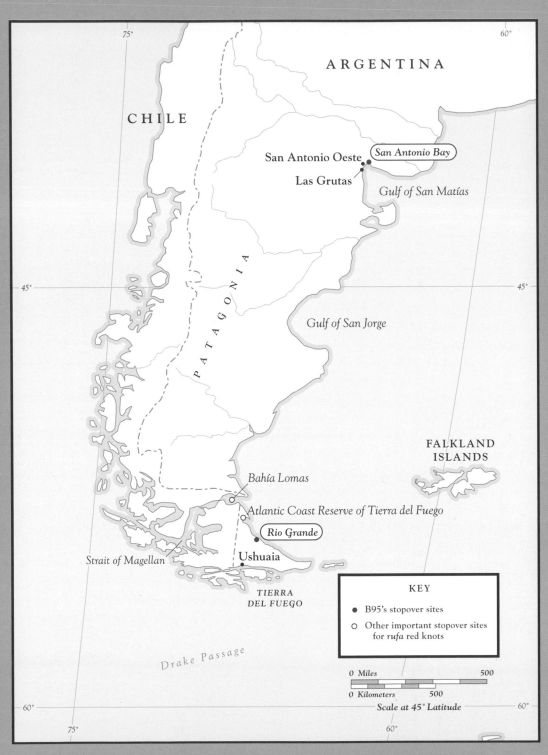

About 60 percent of all *rufa* red knots spend the months of October through February in Patagonia, a region containing the southernmost portion of South America and, even farther south, the islands of Tierra del Fuego. Patagonia is located in Argentina and Chile

Chapter One

SUPERBIRD

October 2009 through February 2010:
Beaches near Rio Grande, Tierra del Fuego, Argentina

To watch the flight of shore birds that have swept up and down the surf lines of the continents for untold thousands of years . . . is to have knowledge of things that are as nearly eternal as any earthly life can be.
—Rachel Carson

DECEMBER 8, 2009, RIO GRANDE, TIERRA DEL FUEGO, ARGENTINA

My laptop says I am 6,811 miles from home. I have just arrived at Rio Grande, a small city in Tierra del Fuego, an archipelago at the southern tip of South America. I'm here to join an international group of scientists in the wintering grounds of *rufa* red knots.

I have never been this far from home. The night before last I slept in the southernmost city in the world, Ushuaia, Argentina, where tourist attractions include penguin watching, glacial hiking, catamaran trips to Antarctica, and the End of the World Museum. Small herds of llamalike guanacos looked up from patches of shrubs as our rental car rattled by. Condors soared high overhead on kitelike wings. Though I am sleep-deprived from twenty-four hours of flying and running to make tight airplane connections, I remind myself that I have traveled barely a third of the distance a red knot flies each year.

Even though it is December everywhere, it is not winter everywhere. *Winter* is a relative term for a bird that spends its year moving along an eighteen-thousand-mile

TIERRA DEL FUEGO: LAND OF FIRE

Rufa red knots have chosen a famously remote place to pass the months October to February. Tierra del Fuego is an archipelago (group of islands) separated from mainland South America by a navigable channel called the Strait of Magellan, featuring bitter winds and treacherous currents. The biggest island, Isla Grande—partly in Chile and partly in Argentina—contains the only two major settlements, Rio Grande and Ushuaia, both in Argentina. In 1520, Ferdinand Magellan, seeking a passage to the spice islands of Asia, passed through the strait and saw fires set by indigenous peoples. He named the land Tierra del Fuego, or "Land of Fire."

In 1831, HMS *Beagle,* with the naturalist Charles Darwin aboard, made a closer study of the land, but the first European colonists did not settle on Tierra del Fuego until 1871. Indigenous peoples quickly died of diseases such as measles and smallpox, against which they had no immunity. Others were imprisoned. Today the main language is Spanish. Ushuaia has become a major tourist destination for adventurers, and is a jumping-off point for Antarctica, some six hundred miles to the south.

I make the acquaintance of a penguin in Tierra del Fuego

circuit throughout the western hemisphere. Here, at the bottom of Argentina, it is austral (meaning southern) summer. Pale light bleeds around my window shade all night long, and by 6:00 a.m. the sun is glaring. A stubborn wind shakes the shrubs outside at all hours and rattles the tin sign out front.

After breeding in the faraway Arctic, thousands of red knots—an estimated 60 percent of the entire *rufa* population—gather here, on the shores of this barren, windswept region, between the months of October and February. I have been invited to join a research team organized by Dr. Allan Baker, professor of ecology and evolutionary biology at the University of Toronto, and Patricia González, a noted Argentine shore-bird biologist. Here in Tierra del Fuego, we will attempt a "catch," banding and studying knots on the Atlantic shoreline near the town of Rio Grande. Because the *rufa* red knot population has crashed so drastically in such a short time, scientists are keen to discover how many knots are here and what percentage of them are juveniles. They're hoping for a higher-than-normal percentage of young birds within a catch, as that would indicate a successful breeding season.

After breakfast, Allan and Patricia announce that we will attempt a catch this very morning. A large flock of knots has been spotted on a beach near the Naval Prefecture—a fortresslike building that functions as a coast guard station—a few miles away. With luck, we'll be able to briefly capture birds with a cannon-fired net, band those not already banded, and record measurements indicating their age, gender, weight, feather condition, bill length, and overall health before releasing them.

We pack up the net, cannons, and assorted instruments and drive to the target beach. The tenacious offshore wind tears at our clothing as we struggle to haul the red-mesh net onto the shore. I climb to a ridge of sand and shield my eyes to squint at the beach and the glittering sea beyond. The tide is halfway out now, but returning rapidly,

WHY DO RED KNOTS GO SO FAR?

"The lives of all wild creatures revolve around food," says Dr. Clive Minton, shorebird expert. "Knots go to the Arctic because there's an incredible volume of food there for a few short weeks. Also, there is enough space up there for each pair to have a separate breeding territory with enough food for their own chicks. And it is light nearly all the time, so they can see their food. It's worth it to risk the hazards of migration to gain that food resource. But they have to be out of there before winter returns in early August.

"Knots have learned to find food along the tidal shores of the world. After breeding, most return to places far south, like Tierra del Fuego. There they can find invertebrate shellfish and worms in the mudflats, and since it is summer there, they have plenty of daylight to see their prey.

"If you could ban birds from the southern hemisphere, there wouldn't be enough food to support them in the north. So they've learned to spread out. And by spreading out, they've maximized the world population of their species."

(TOP) A sweeping view of the restinga country of Patagonia
(BOTTOM) A close-up of restinga, the pits and pocks of which contain protein-rich mussel spat

channels filling with water. The exposed ocean floor is unlike anything I have ever seen. It looks like a pavement composed of flat, overlapping reddish-brown shelves that are pocked with thousands of holes still gleaming with water from the last high tide.

Experts say the lure of Tierra del Fuego to red knots—the reason they fly all this way—is the food locked within this seascape. The seafloor here is called *restinga*, formed when reddish dust swept seaward by the wind off the treeless plains is packed down into a hard pavement by the weight of the tides. Throughout the restinga shelves lie dense beds of mussels, whose young are known as spat. Their shells are not yet fully formed, making them soft enough for knots to digest. The spat are just strong enough to cling to the

B95: *CALIDRIS CANUTUS RUFA*

In 1753 the Swedish biologist Carl von Linné, better known as Linnaeus, developed a system that gave every species of plant and animal in the world a unique sequence of Latin names. The framework had seven parts. A red knot belongs to the kingdom Animalia—the animal kingdom—and the phylum Chordata—meaning it has a spine with vertebrae. Like all birds, knots are of the class Aves. They belong to the order Charadriiformes—a large group of shorebirds with 16 families and 314 species—and to the family Scolopacidae, shorebirds with long legs and bills, and slender bodies. The genus is *Calidris*—sandpipers of the seashore and tundra. Linnaeus himself named the species *canutus* after the Danish king Canute, who was said to be so powerful that he could hold back the tides with a simple command.

There are six red knot subspecies, named *rogersi*, *piersmai*, *canutus*, *roselaari*, *islandica*, and *rufa*. B95 belongs to *rufa*—meaning "red." Scientists believe all six subspecies came from a single red knot species that lived near the North Pole until the earth's climate got so cold that they were forced to migrate southward to warmer places. Over thousands of years they sorted themselves into six different migratory routes, until they became permanently separated into subspecies. As of this writing, *rufa* is the only one of the six red knot subspecies with a population crashing toward extinction.

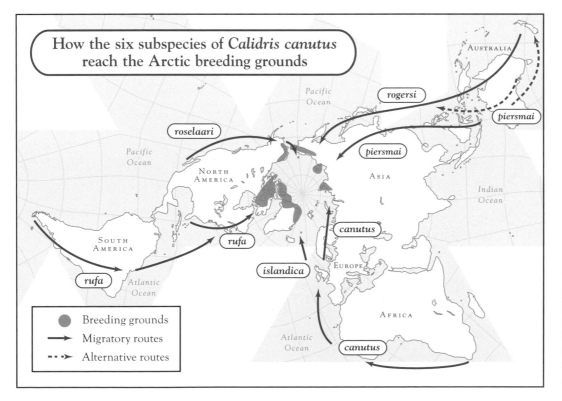

How the six subspecies of *Calidris canutus* reach the Arctic breeding grounds

Breeding grounds
Migratory routes
Alternative routes

The globe-spanning migration routes of the red knot's six subspecies. They converge within the Arctic Circle during breeding season, though even then each subspecies maintains a separate territory restinga as waves wash over them, but no match for the tug of a ravenous red knot's bill. Red knots work the pitted restinga shelves quickly during low tide, picking off spat with mechanical efficiency and also feeding on populations of worms and clams that peak here between November and January.

There's another reason that Tierra del Fuego lures *rufa* knots: daylight is almost constant here at this time of year. Because there are more hours of daylight at this extreme southern latitude than, say, the typical twelve hours at the equator, birds have more time to see their prey. So in Tierra del Fuego food is often uncovered by seawater and in plain sight during two low tides instead of just one. Here, the birds not only have more food, but more time to find it.

One reason for the excitement the shorebird researchers and I feel, as we finally attach the long net to the rockets that will propel it, is the chance to meet the most famous shorebird in the world. The legendary B95 has been captured four times, always on the restinga of Rio Grande during austral summer. We can almost feel his presence. As we conceal ourselves in nearby beach grass and wait hopefully for the cannons' muffled roar, many of us wonder: Can B95 still be alive?

1995: THE BLACK BAND

B95 made his debut to science on February 20, 1995, within sight of where we are right now. That year, a Canadian research team, organized and led by Dr. Baker, flew to Tierra del Fuego to band red knots. Baker wondered why these birds would bother to fly so far each year and what their exact routes were. How had these pathways developed? Some of Dr. Baker's Toronto colleagues balked at traveling great distances to trap birds in the wild. They preferred instead to learn the old-fashioned way—by shooting birds when they came through Canada and then examining the dead creatures as specimens in a laboratory. Dr. Baker made it clear that he would have none of it. "I said to them, 'How can you talk about conservation biology when you are killing thousands of animals?'"

Dr. Baker took to the field—unarmed. He devoted his energy to trapping knots briefly and marking individuals with lightweight, color-coded leg bands—and then releasing them. If researchers could band enough shorebirds and see them again and again at various places throughout their migratory circuit, the pathways and stopping places would become apparent. The more birds they could catch and band—and then release—the more data would pile up and the more clues they would have.

But red knots are very hard to catch. Knots aren't like ducks, which can be baited with bread crumbs or decoyed in. They are notoriously wary. They feed, sleep, and travel in cliquishly tight flocks. While feeding they post sentinels, birds that send the whole flock flashing away with one warning cry. Dr. Baker hoped to catch at least three hundred knots, but he didn't know how. To increase his chances, his team flew in the famed Dr. Clive Minton from Australia. Minton, a metals scientist by profession, had spent much of his life perfecting techniques to trap shorebirds. He pioneered the art of using cannons to shoot rockets attached to

A worker frees a knot from a cannon net

nets over the feeding flocks. After decades of experimentation, Dr. Minton had become the unquestioned world expert. If anyone could catch red knots, Clive Minton could.

Because the early-morning air was unusually warm, workers stripped to their shorts and T-shirts. At ten o'clock the incoming tide pushed a huge group of shorebirds squarely into target range. Dr. Minton fired off his tennis-court-size net, which whizzed through the air and came down upon a mammoth group of shorebirds, mostly red knots. It was a spectacular catch, much bigger than they had anticipated. Team members sprinted through the sand and plunged into the surf to gather up the front edge of the net and save the trapped birds from drowning.

It took two hours just to untangle all the birds, during which time the temperature steadily dropped. Local teenagers jumped in to help carry birds to cloth-covered cages where they would remain calm until they were measured, weighed, and released. By the third hour the researchers were shivering in wet clothes. A violent storm welled up, pelting everyone with hailstones that soon turned to snowflakes. Freezing workers struggled to move their stiff, numb fingers enough to band the birds, take measurements, and record data.

The Argentine navy sent two canvas-covered trucks out to the beach so that the scientists could climb in and finish their work. They labored for hours in a crouched position, their backs bent under the low roof. The team captured so many birds that they quickly ran out of colored bands. Improvising, they fired up a camp stove to heat thin strips of black plastic found in one of the trucks until the strips were pliable enough to bend into bands. Repeatedly scorching their fingers on the stove's flame, the researchers carefully wrapped the black strips around each bird's lower right leg and joined the end with a soldering iron. They also applied a yellow band to the lower left leg.

The bird we know as B95 was among 850 red knots caught that day. His now-iconic black band was applied to his lower right leg by a shivering worker with stiff fingers and an aching back. Of the hundreds of knots that received black bands in the trucks that day, he is the lone survivor that scientists can identify. Records show that this knot had adult plumage even then, which means he had to have been at least three years old in 1995, and could have been older.

MOLT

The process of exchanging used and worn flight feathers for new feathers is called *molt*. A knot's feathers are replaced in a regular sequence. *Primary feathers*—the long feathers on the outside portion of the wing—are replaced feather by feather from the inside out. *Secondary feathers*—those closer to the body—are replaced from the outside in. The feathers die and regrow in a careful order, so that the bird always has enough feathers to fly. It takes about sixty days for a knot to replace its primary feathers. Flight feathers are renewed once a year and body feathers twice, first in autumn to produce the gray winter plumage, and again in spring to create a bright red breeding plumage.

This red knot, captured in the fall, is just starting primary molt (from innermost primary outward) by shedding worn (pale brown) flight feathers and starting to grow new, blood-filled "pin" feathers

2001: AN IDENTITY

Six years later, on November 17, 2001, one of the black-banded birds from 1995 was snared in a cannon net catch, just miles from where he was originally caught. Both bands were still on his legs. Patricia González added a new flag to his upper left leg, bearing the inscription B95. "On that day we used laser-inscribed flags for the first time," recalls González. "We inscribed one letter and two numbers on each band to give each individual bird a distinct identity. The figures were big and clear and easy to read through a spotting scope. We used up all one hundred of the bands in series A and we still had more birds to band, so we started the B series. This bird got a flag reading B95. The 95 doesn't represent the year he was caught. We just happened to be at that number when we banded him. It's a coincidence that '95 was the year when he was first captured."

2003: A SURVIVOR

Now he was—and always would be—B95. And when he turned up again at Tierra del Fuego in 2003 it was clear he was more than just an extraordinary pilot who could find his way back year after year. He was a survivor, for the entire *rufa* subspecies of red knots was plunging toward extinction. Researchers in the United States, Chile, Canada, Brazil, and Argentina were all reporting significantly fewer knots. Some estimates indicated that *half* of all adult birds had died in just two years, between 2000 and 2002. Yet in 2003, B95, at least eleven years old, was still completing marathon migratory flights. Something about this bird was exceptional; he seemed to possess some extraordinary combination of physical toughness, navigational skill, judgment, and luck.

2007: THE MOONBIRD

B95 was captured again in Tierra del Fuego six years later, on November 8, 2007. Once the birds were freed from the net, researchers assembled into teams and began to band, weigh, and measure them. Each team worked efficiently in brilliant sunlight and said little beyond the statistics they were reporting.

BANDS AND FLAGS

Bands are lightweight rings that fit around bird legs, allowing observers to see that birds have been captured before and, more recently, to know, through color-coding, the country in which they were first captured.

Flags are bands with tabs sticking out, on which combinations of letters and numbers may be inscribed (such as B95) so that each individual bird has an identity. Inscribed flags allow observers to identify a bird from a distance through binoculars or spotting scopes without having to capture it. Five Western nations participate in a color-coded shorebird flag scheme: Canada (yellow), the United States (green), Brazil (blue), Argentina (orange), and Chile (red).

Banding authorities recommend that the total weight of all bands, rings, and tracking devices should not exceed 4 percent of a bird's weight.

B95, as he appeared in his gray nonbreeding plumage at Rio Grande, November 8, 2007

That changed when Allan Baker was heard to mutter the words "My God." Everyone looked up. Dr. Baker was holding a knot between his thumb and forefinger at arm's length and staring intently at it.

"I looked down and there was the black flag of the 1995 catch and the band inscribed B95," he recalls. "I couldn't believe I was holding him." In the twelve years since Dr. Baker had first met this bird, his own hair had whitened. But B95 looked ageless. "He was in fantastic condition," Dr. Baker recalls. "His weight was where it should be. He had wonderful plumage. He was as fit as a three-year-old. I was holding a superbird in my hand."

Researchers scrambled to their feet and clustered around. Some went for cameras. Patricia González, an expert on the development of bird feathers, remembers feeling guilty for leaving her post, but she couldn't help it. Here in Dr. Baker's grasp was the Moonbird, as B95 was now called by shorebird enthusiasts, a feathered veteran of thirty or more migratory flights between the bottom of the world and the top.

But there was more to it than that. "He was *alive*," remembers González, her voice catching in the telling. "Still alive."

When B95 was born, on an Arctic day long ago, he was one of an estimated 150,000 *rufa* red knots. Now the world population was far less than half that number. Some were predicting *rufa's* extinction within the next five years unless something could be done quickly.

After recording B95's measurements, Allan Baker handed him carefully to Patricia González. She examined the condition of B95's plumage, now gray and white instead of the red of his breeding season, and checked the progress of his molt, which had not yet begun at this early date. She inserted a thin needle beneath his wing and drew a small quantity of blood, which would later confirm that B95 is a male.

The bird remained calm in González's grasp, even though her hands were trembling as she worked. "I kept talking to him," she remembers. "I kept saying, 'Forgive me, please, I won't hurt you. I will release you soon.' The heat of his tiny body was warming my hands and his heart was beating so fast. As I was working, I kept wondering, 'How can such a fragile thing be so powerful?'"

González noticed that B95 had lost the original yellow band from his lower left leg. She replaced it with an orange band—orange for Argentina. When she finished, the bird had an orange flag with B95 on his upper left leg, an orange band on his lower left leg, and the old black flag on the lower right leg.

She took a long, final look at him before releasing him. What stories he could tell! How had this small creature made it through so many storms? How had he avoided the falcon's chopping dive every single time?

These photos show how to correctly record the sighting of a banded shorebird. If you see B95 on a beach, you would note the following information: REKN, indicating that he is a red knot; FO (B95) for his orange flag, inscribed B95; O for an orange band; b for a black band; and a dash indicating that there is nothing on his upper right leg. You would report his full record as

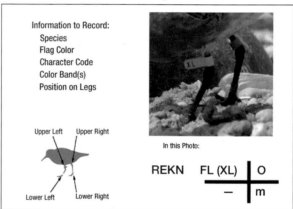

The colors of flags used to mark shorebirds within the western hemisphere

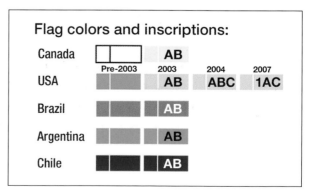

I record the weight of a "recaptured" knot. The orange band on the bird's upper left leg shows that, like B95, it was first captured in Argentina

Above all, how had he managed to stay alive when so many others had fallen?

Patricia González knew she had to let him go. She adjusted the bands and flags on his legs, held him out toward the sea, and opened her hands. He fluttered for a moment to right himself in the air, regained control of his powerful wings, then flew off on a sharp curve to the right and disappeared.

Now, two years later, here I am crouching in Argentine beach grass with a small group of scientists and volunteers, waiting for the cannon's boom and hoping to meet B95. When it sounds, we run zigzagging through the trash-strewn beach grass and sprint out onto the shore. We scoop the front of the net from the water to free the teeming, writhing, chattering birds. We spend the rest of the day banding them, measuring bills and wings, drawing blood to determine gender, and recording statistics that will later be computerized.

In the end, we catch 156 knots. Twenty-six are "retraps," meaning they have been captured before and are already banded. About 25 percent of the birds are juveniles, with yellow legs and white crescents beneath gray feathers. They have just completed the first half of their rookie circuit around the western hemisphere. Almost all the flags are Argentine orange, but none says B95. Where is he? Did he manage to wiggle out under the net? Is he foraging just down the beach? Has he decided to stay farther north this season? Or has his time finally come?

Allan Baker and Patricia González decide that one good catch is enough for the season. They don't want to stress these birds any further or divert them from the important work they have to do each and every day to prepare for their upcoming journey north. With no remaining chance to capture B95, our only hope is that a sharp-eyed observer will spot him through a beach telescope. Given that thousands of knots are spread out over miles and miles of beaches and flats in Tierra del Fuego, the odds seem minuscule.

I fly back to the United States on Monday, December 14, and immediately begin typing up my notes. As I sit at my computer, I hear the faint bell indicating an e-mail message. Looking up, I see it's from Patricia González, with the subject "Un Viejo amigo," Spanish for "an old friend."

It begins: "Yesterday morning while scanning for red knots at Malvinas Memorial Monument, we saw B95. As all the birds were moving very fast, at first I did not realize he was there, but then, when I could see the combination of bands, can you not imagine what joy I felt!"

I push my chair back and let the message wash over me. He is still alive. While so many other *rufa* red knots have disappeared, B95 is in Tierra del Fuego, just as he always is at this time of year, plucking spat off the restinga shelves, preening his new flight feathers into flight-readiness, practicing snap-the-whip formation flying with the others, and getting ready for another flight north that no other knot knows better how to make. He has survived another year of marathon flights and now, nearly eighteen years of age, is getting ready for perhaps his most challenging flight yet. "Superbird" indeed. That's not the half of it: this bird has to be among the toughest four ounces of life in the world.

Clive Minton holds two eastern
curlews—the largest shorebirds
in the world

CLIVE MINTON
Shorebird Pioneer

In the summer of 1950 while bicycling on a beach in the north of England, sixteen-year-old Clive Minton came upon a shorebird running in circles in the sand. The tame bird let Clive pick it up, but even at eye level he couldn't identify it. Frustrated, he pedaled it to the renowned shorebird expert Dr. Eric Ennion, who had a research station up the beach. Dr. Ennion instantly identified it as a sanderling. "It's a juvenile," he said. "It must have flown in from its breeding grounds in Greenland overnight."

It was the beginning of a strong partnership. Fueled by a common passion for shorebirds, Dr. Ennion and Clive Minton teamed up to develop ways to trap and band enough shorebirds (called "waders" in Britain) to discover their migration paths. Shorebirds were notoriously wary and very hard to trap. For the next ten summers Clive led a battalion of his schoolmates to the beach to experiment with traps. They began with the ponderous "clap net," mounted on a hinged stake and dragged out to the shore. When a bird wandered near, a concealed birder pulled a string, which sprung the net. They caught exactly one bird the first time. "It was the birth of shorebird banding in Britain," says Minton.

They built bigger and bigger clap nets, which just got slower and slower. Next they tried "mist nets," stretched out across a beach at night. They caught more birds, but still not enough to learn much.

In 1959 Minton borrowed a gigantic rocket-propelled net that had been used to catch wild geese. The net was so big that it took nearly a dozen workers just to set it up. Six rockets, each weighing 30 pounds, were electrically connected up with a special charge of cordite—a slow-burning smokeless propellant—and tied to the colossal net. On August 18, 1959, Minton's crew blasted the net over a beach in Northumberland, trapping 1,100 shorebirds. It was by far the biggest shorebird harvest in world history, producing almost immediate gains in knowledge. One red knot banded that day in England was discovered more than three thousand miles away in West Africa only five days later.

In 1966 Minton developed his own cannon net, using black powder as a propellant. The first test was almost the last. "One projectile sailed over a field, cleared some distant trees, and headed straight toward a farmhouse on the main road," recalls Minton. "Then there was the most almighty crash! I thought, *My God, have I put it through the roof?* I leaped into my car and drove down the road about a quarter mile. There was a huge branch of an elm tree down in the middle of a road, but the farmhouse was untouched. If the projectile had hit the house, that might have stopped the program right there, but it missed."

Decade by decade, Clive Minton kept fine-tuning his cannon nets until he developed many of the models and procedures now used to learn about shorebirds throughout the world.

Fourteen-year-old Clive Minton with a grey heron that had fallen from its nest. Minton nursed it back to health, taking it on the handlebars of his bicycle to a local gravel pit to fish each day

This map depicts what may be the first two legs of B95's northbound migration flight. He has never been seen or trapped at San Antonio Bay or at Lagoa do Peixe, but both are well-known stopover sites for knots northbound from lower Patagonia

Chapter Two

THE FLIGHT MACHINE

Mid-March to Mid-May: Argentina, Brazil, and the United States

Human ingenuity may make various inventions, but it will never devise any inventions more beautiful, nor more simple, nor more to the purpose than Nature does; because in her inventions nothing is wanting and nothing is superfluous.   —Leonardo da Vinci

THE BODYBUILDER

How can B95 fly so far? The secret is an astounding feat of bodybuilding. During the last weeks of February and the beginning of March, he transforms himself from a feeding machine into a flight machine. It all begins with the simple, powerful urge to *go*. Because of a secretion of hormones—chemicals that control the activity of cells and organs that direct behavior—B95 becomes more restless as the amount of light in the sky decreases day by day. With every ounce of his being, he wants to move north.

B95's ultimate destination is a patch of wiry grass and bleached rock within the central Canadian Arctic—about nine thousand miles away. Right now that place is smothered in snowdrifts, its ponds locked in ice, but by the time he arrives—*if* he can make it again—the Arctic will be bursting with food, color, and light. There he will seek a mate and, with luck, produce hatchlings once again. But this trip is too long to take without stopping; a robin-size knot cannot pack enough fuel for the whole journey. To keep from starving, he'll have to divide his flight into segments, stopping at refueling stations along the way.

In the weeks before liftoff, B95 tries to satisfy his ravenous hunger. As he gobbles down row after row of mussel spat, his body quickly converts the food into fat, the ideal flight fuel since a gram of fat contains about eight times more energy than a gram of protein. Fat also releases water to his body during flight so that he won't have to stop to drink. Studies show that fat birds fly faster than thin birds, and can stay in the air longer.

SNAPPING THE WHIP

Red knots perform acrobatic group flights, with hundreds of birds flying tightly together at high speeds, rushing back and forth, up and down, flashing colors as if controlled by a single mind. They seem to practice these flights during their "winter" months in Tierra del Fuego. One explanation is that the group flights are evasive maneuvers meant to confuse predators, especially falcons that patrol the cliffs behind the restinga beaches of Patagonia. A falcon seeks to pick and harry one bird out of a flock. But if the flock flies as one constantly shifting organism—now a ball, now a rippling blanket, flashing white, then brown, offering no one individual up as a target—perhaps every member of the flock can escape. The shorebird scientist Brian Harrington saw one such flight involving three thousand knots, rising and falling along a line in tight choreography. "[It] reminded me of the snap of a whip," he wrote.

A chubby knot, almost ready for liftoff

Eating constantly when he can find food, B95 seems to inflate, storing fat in cavities and compartments all over his body. His stomach and digestive organs expand so that he can take in even more fuel. (A red knot can consume fourteen times its own weight. To do that, a human weighing 110 pounds would need to eat 2,300 hamburgers at two thirds of a pound per hamburger, with cheese and tomato.)

B95 stuffs himself until the last few days before departure—and then he switches gears. He eats softer food, and less of it, and the internal organs he won't need during flight begin to shrink. His liver and gut shrivel, as do the muscles in his legs. His gizzard—an organ that grinds food—decreases in size by nearly half, meaning he will be able to eat only soft food when he stops to refuel. By the time he is finished making these changes, he has reduced his body mass by nearly 30 percent. His body is now packed with fuel, without carrying a gram of baggage. He sports a deeper chest—containing a heart newly enlarged to pump more blood to his bulked-up flight muscles. The sinews of his breast muscles have toughened into tissues that are among the strongest in the animal kingdom.

Goodbye to Patagonia

In his final hours at Rio Grande, B95 is a flight machine, nervously pacing the beach and yanking up final scraps of mussel spat to top off the tank. Bulked up and loaded with fuel, he is ready again to face any challenge a flight can offer.

LIFTOFF

When a front passes over Tierra del Fuego in the late afternoon and the wind shifts abruptly to the north, B95 and the rest of the flock stir. Some birds produce shrill calls that seem to rally the birds together. Then hundreds of chattering birds, some beginning to show hints of red in their feathering, beat their wings and rise into the air as one, towering up into a tight, swirling, shape-shifting column that seeks the wind and looks like drifting smoke to a shorebound observer.

The flock sweeps back and forth through the air a few times, seeming to take bearings and set internal instruments before committing to a definite course. Once it does, the birds cleave the air with deep, rhythmic strokes, several beats a second. They labor to fly fast now, for their wings must keep huge loads of fuel aloft. If they fly too slowly, the burden will be too much, their wings will fail, and they will fall.

As B95 flies, each wing beat is a series of precisely coordinated actions involving all the individual feathers in both wings. The downstroke propels him forward and the upstroke pushes his feathers against the air to create lift. B95 and the others climb steadily, seeking high, thin air where resistance is light. A strong tailwind boosts their speed, adding 10 miles per hour. Before long, the flock is outpacing the automobiles that crawl along the Patagonian coastline far below.

B95 and the other knots assume a V formation, exchanging leaders frequently, some birds drafting in the wake of others. Neighboring wings almost touch with each stroke. With each flap, circular air currents called vortices arise a few inches from the wingtip on both the downstroke and the up, boosting each bird's individual power with contributions from nearby birds. Like a rippling flag of energy, the flock climbs higher and higher through the air, birds chattering as they fly.

They race through the late afternoon and into evening. Andean mountain peaks shine against a golden sunset on their left, and the Atlantic Ocean scrolls out to the horizon on their right. The sound of surf pounding against the shoreline rumbles up from far below them. Rising into cool, thin air where flight reaches maximum efficiency, they settle in for the long night of flying ahead.

A FLYING COMPASS

B95 flies with a strong, rapid, steady rhythm hour after hour, drawing down fuel as he goes. He knows where he is in the air, and has no trouble staying on course even in the darkness of night.

The prowess of long-distance travelers like B95 makes human observers wonder: How do migrating birds navigate? How can they fly so far, yet manage to return to the same place year after year at exactly the right time? There have been many experiments to try to find out. Some studies suggest that migratory shorebirds such as B95 are born with inherited flight plans that guide their first long flights. According to this explanation—which not all scientists accept—during the year of his first Great Circuit around the hemisphere, B95 was guided by a preset, genetically controlled inner map. This "software" instructed him to fly in a certain direction for a certain length of time, then to change to another course for another preset length of time, and to keep on making these time and direction changes until, zigzagging through the sky on automatic pilot, he arrived at his destination.

B95 may have also gained information by traveling with more experienced knots that first year, but juvenile knots often fly in flocks only with other young birds. First-time flights are hazardous: many young knots are blown off course by strong winds or sudden storms, become separated from the flock, and cannot find their way back.

Knots use the stars, the sun, the earth's magnetic field, and the ability to recognize landforms, among other things, to guide them on their long journeys

Isolated and inexperienced, some of these birds cannot locate food and starve. Slightly more than half of all *rufa* red knots die in their first year of life. B95 was luckier than many: he made it through his first year. Perhaps he had a knack for making safe decisions from the very start. Some scientists have suggested that maybe he knows how to keep himself within the safety of the middle of the flock.

By the time B95 had completed his first Great Circuit, he had learned a great deal. He came to understand where the sun should be at any time of the day. This is not a matter of knowledge—he can't tell time—but of instinct or intuition. If it was early in the day—perhaps the time that humans would know as 7:00 a.m.—B95 could recognize that the sun should be in the east, just a little bit above the horizon. To head north, the flock would have to keep the sun on the right.

He also learned to use the movement of stars to guide him at night. In the northern hemisphere, the North Star's position remains constant, while all other stars seem to move around it. This gave him information by which to steer through the sky. He probably used landmarks such as mountains, rivers, and coastlines to ascertain his position. He could even pick up on changes in the earth's magnetic field as he flew along, giving him a sensory map to use in combination with other systems. By his second Great Circuit, B95 was a flying compass.

Now B95 streaks through the darkness, working his breast muscles like pistons hour after hour, chattering signals into the collective brain of the flock and gaining information in return. The journey is exhausting and dangerous. Some knots won't make it. But with wisdom and experience honed over nearly two decades of aviation, B95 helps keep the flock on a steady course as it races through the Patagonian night toward the first refueling station.

FIRST STOP

San Antonio Bay—nine hundred miles north of Rio Grande

After two days and nights of continuous flying, B95 spots the reddish smear of the first restinga shelf he has seen since he left Rio Grande. That can only mean one thing: good food and plenty of it. The message transmits through the flock: we're going down. Wave after wave of hungry knots tuck their wings and plummet down onto a wide beach, curved wings raised as they meet the ground and stagger to a halt.

B95 sets upon the local menu at once, ravenously pulling spat from restinga shelves, wolfing down five to ten mussels per minute. There seems to be no limit to the larder at San Antonio Bay. At low tide, the moon draws the ocean four miles back from the shore, exposing a vast intertidal zone bursting—like an overflowing banquet—with worms, clams, mussels, and small crustaceans.

The beaches at San Antonio are popular with another species, too—humans. One sandy stretch known as Las Grutas has become the second-most-popular beach destination in all of Patagonia. Peak beach season is in January, but even now, on a warm, sunny afternoon in late March, Las Grutas attracts beachcombers, hovering gulls, Frisbee-fetching dogs, four-wheel-drive beach vehicles, and shorebirds. B95 does his best to concentrate and maintain his feeding position on the shoreline, but he and his flock mates are bumped off by one bigger creature after another. It's more than an annoyance. It means constantly having to fly out over the water and settle somewhere else along the beach. It burns fuel he has just banked. It's like taking two steps forward and one step back.

SECOND STOP

Lagoa do Peixe, Brazil—one thousand miles northeast of San Antonio Bay

Still, after a few days feeding at San Antonio, B95 is blubbery once again and itching to move on. When a northerly wind arises, the flock lifts off, climbs through the clouds, and closes into cruising formation. Now it banks slightly and shadows the Atlantic coastline northeastward through Argentina and Uruguay and into Brazil. After one thousand miles of nonstop flight, the knots recognize a wide blue lagoon fringed by blazing white dunes of sand on the east and linked by channels to the ocean. This is Lagoa do Peixe, in southeastern Brazil—second stop. The knots land at the lagoon's south end, where a constant wind has scoured the water pan-shallow—only an inch or so deep. It is another ancient food treasure. Here a knot can spend day after day wading knee-deep in clear salty water, snatching up small snails that are abundant and easy to find.

The shallow lagoon is so flat and wide—ten miles across in some places—that it makes a perfect place for the flock to roost at night. Many wild animals sleep in hidden places—squirming under rocks or backing into caves or slipping behind a curtain of leaves—but not red knots. A knot's defense against predators is vigilance—a screamed

Lagoa do Peixe, a likely second stop on B95's northbound flight

(ABOVE) Often working at night, researchers at Lagoa do Peixe attempt to catch migrating knots in free-standing mist nets
(RIGHT) A red knot captured in a mist net at night, Lagoa do Peixe

alarm and swift evasion. At night, red knots stand bunched together out in the open, on beaches or flat areas of mud above the reach of high tide, scanning for predators in all directions. They know that if they can just get their wings moving before a predator reaches them, they will have the advantage.

Tonight, as the wind rises, B95 stands on one leg in the shallow lagoon, surrounded closely by his flock mates. He tucks his bill under a wing, but he doesn't drop his guard. B95 sleeps with one eye open. So do the others. A roosting flock of knots is like a single organism equipped with hundreds of eyes and ears. Light sleepers, they instantly detect

Roosting knots sleep on one leg with one eye open, ever alert for danger

the feathery rush of an air attack from a falcon or an owl, or the splash of a fisherman's dog. A warning cry from one sentinel sends the whole flock flashing away in less than a heartbeat.

B95 lingers with the flock for several weeks in Lagoa do Peixe, snatching up snails by day and dozing in the lagoon at night, moving around very little. He converts protein to fat until, by the first of May, he is chubby and restless and his hormones are telling him to

THE MARATHON ROUTE NORTH

Shorebird scientists know that a marathon flight between Lagoa do Peixe and Delaware Bay is possible. On May 15, 1984, Brian Harrington found several banded red knots at Delaware Bay that he had seen as fat birds at Lagoa do Peixe in Brazil only days before. Even stronger proof came when a red knot tracked by a new light-sensitive device called a geolocator left northern Brazil on May 19, 2010, and arrived at Delaware Bay on May 23 after having flown four days and nights without stopping.

The long route may be the preferred route for many knots. Some of the highest weights ever recorded for red knots have come from birds captured at Lagoa do Peixe in the hours just before the flight north. These birds, described by one observer as "ripe peaches," seemed fueled up to travel a great distance. Most likely they were ready to blast out over the Amazon rain forest, abandon the South American coastline for the blue Atlantic, and stroke their way up the U.S. Atlantic shoreline until the familiar shape of Delaware Bay appeared below them.

fly again. His next destination is a critical one: Delaware Bay, midway up the Atlantic coast of the United States. That's the last fuel stop before the final push to his Arctic breeding grounds. But since the food he expects to find at Delaware Bay will be available for only two short weeks, between the middle and the end of May, he needs to arrive on time. His inner clock pushes him to get going.

But what route to take? Delaware Bay is an enormous distance from Lagoa do Peixe—nearly five thousand miles, more than half the entire northbound flight. He *could* try to make it in one nonstop journey. That would mean several days of continually stroking his wings without food, water, or rest. Or he could hopscotch his way up the northern coast of South America and get closer to the United States before taking off over the water. Or he could even chop the flight up, flying to a Caribbean island before continuing on to North America. But that would take time.

Whatever his choice, this leg of the journey will be a severe challenge. Some knots will run out of fuel and drop exhausted from the sky. Others will burn muscle in the final hours of flight and arrive at Delaware Bay panting for oxygen, with bones protruding, desperate for food. B95 will likely start out on a path that has worked before, improvise along the way if necessary, and try to make it work again.

THE PEREGRINE FALCON

The peregrine falcon, *Falco peregrinus*, is found from the restinga of Patagonia to the monumental islands of Mingan. And everywhere along the way it strikes terror into the hearts of shorebirds. The peregrine is a deadly hunter with tapering wings and a distinctive black teardrop below each eye. No hawk is faster—or more athletic. The peregrine tracks its prey by lifting itself above other birds and then folding its wings to "stoop" down on them, plunging through the air at speeds of up to 200 miles per hour. Often the chase ends with the falcon neatly shearing a panic-stricken victim's head off in midair with a single stroke of its talons.

The ultimate predator, a peregrine falcon carries home a willet snatched from the air

Patricia González inspects the feathers of a knot captured at San Antonio

PATRICIA GONZÁLEZ
Protecting the Beaches of San Antonio

Biologist Patricia González is head of the wetlands program of Fundación Inalafquen in San Antonio Bay, Argentina. She travels throughout the world, studying knots along their migratory circuit. She placed the orange flag on B95's left leg that gives him his unique identity.

After college, González explored the marshes and beaches around her as a young girl. At the age of ten she read a book about the destruction of the world's forests. It turned her into a conservationist. "I thought, *Wow, how can adults be so dumb? We have to find a solution.*" She came to know and love birds only after a pair of eyeglasses corrected her severe nearsightedness and she could finally see them.

After college, González was hired by the city of San Antonio to produce a study of the birds using the beaches of San Antonio Bay. Her data would help city officials decide whether a proposed factory should be built on the beach. They wanted to know: How many birds were there? During which months did they gather? Where were their favorite feeding beaches and roosting areas? González discovered that San Antonio attracted great numbers of shorebirds during spring and fall migration. The bay's huge intertidal zone provided the large quantities of food they needed to fuel their journeys.

Reporting her data, González recommended a series of steps to protect the birds at the beaches. But few city officials listened. "I heard the word *chorlito* directed at me," she recalls. "Where I come from that means 'stupid.'"

Patricia González was anything but stupid, and she had resources of her own. "By then I was a high school teacher," she says. "I had smart students. We got to work. We censused birds every year. We developed a mathematical analysis so we could prove how important this place is." González and her students wrote a blizzard of letters pressing political leaders to protect the beaches. In 1993 they took a bus to the provincial capital, Viedma, to support a bill to create the Bahía de San Antonio Natural Protected Area. González's students presented powerful testimony supported by compelling data. The bill was passed.

González didn't stop there. She continued to fight for shorebird habitat at San Antonio. She worked hard to improve her English so that she could present papers at international conferences. She developed a special knowledge of feather development. During banding operations it is often she who insists that birds be held properly—with legs dangling freely—and released promptly. Year by year she recruited more people to count shorebirds at San Antonio, publishing the results, until the bay became recognized as one of the hemisphere's most important places for migratory shorebirds—especially red knots.

"I am completely in love with the red knot," she says. "It is exciting to be part of a worldwide network dedicated to understanding and saving this bird. And holding B95 in my hands—several times? This is among the biggest thrills of my life."

Chapter Three

SHOWDOWN AT DELAWARE BAY

Last two weeks in May: Delaware Bay, United States

When one tugs at a single thing in nature, he finds it attached to the rest of the world.

—John Muir

NIGHT OF A FULL MOON IN MID-MAY

Wave by wave, ocean water climbs up over the beaches of Delaware Bay, steadily narrowing aprons of sand. Each wave paints the beach with a fringe of hissing foam before it retreats. And each dying wave uncovers a glistening army of prehistoric-looking creatures marching onto the beach from out of the dark water. They are horseshoe crabs—males attached to females by means of a special limb. Thousands of crabs push forward, jostling for choice positions on the exposed sand.

Finding a good spot, a female crab—much larger than the male—squirms into the sand and deposits a cluster of about four thousand tiny green eggs. Once finished, she rises, advances a few steps, and positions the male—or often several males—over the pit she has dug so that he can fertilize the eggs. Then she covers the eggs with sand and backs up. As the tide recedes, she repeats the process again and again during the night. By the end of spawning season, each female will have laid nearly eighty thousand eggs. The beach will be saturated with eggs, most buried in the sand but some visible in dark rows that trace the shapes of last night's waves. At this point, some crabs are so exhausted that they can't make it back into the ocean. They lie like hubcaps on the beach, some overturned, legs flailing, lancelike tails waving in the air.

Daylight the next morning finds the same beach teeming with action. Crying gulls wheel overhead. B95, mixed in with a flock of chattering red knots, ruddy turnstones, sanderlings, and other shorebirds, jabs his bill with pistonlike speed into the sand to gorge on the banquet of fresh horseshoe crab eggs. No single feeding spot on earth

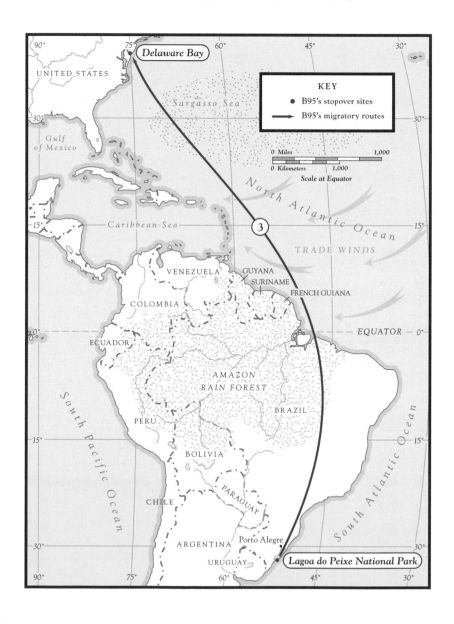

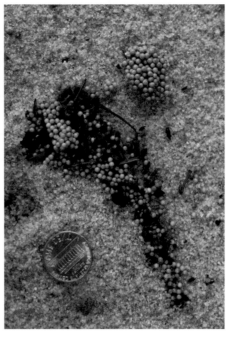

(ABOVE) A male horseshoe crab is attached to a female during a full-moon spawn
(RIGHT) Clusters of tiny globes—horseshoe crab eggs—are the prime fuel for Arctic-bound knots. By the end of a successful spawn, each female will have laid thousands of eggs
(BOTTOM RIGHT) By the end, some crabs are too exhausted to make it back into the water

offers more fuel in less time than the beaches that ring this huge bay, immediately recognizable to a knot from the air.

The payoff is fast. Not long ago B95 was burning muscle just to stay alive in the final hours of his journey from South America. Now, head down, raking in green eggs for hours at a time, skipping expertly to the next beach when the oncoming tide covers up a feeding spot, B95 quickly begins to build his fat back up. He can eat more than eight thousand soft, easy-to-digest eggs in a single day if he can find them. Feeding steadily, B95 can double his weight in two weeks. With luck, by the time his feathers fluff with the wind that will lift him north once again toward his breeding grounds, he'll have taken on enough fuel to make the entire two-thousand-mile trip to the Arctic. To ensure survival, he'll need to have a bit left over, for the ground in the Far North may still be covered with snow and the tundra ponds may still be frozen.

The horseshoe crab eggs at Delaware Bay give B95 and other red knots a chance to

DELAWARE BAY

Delaware Bay is a fifty-two-mile-long inlet of the Atlantic Ocean, located about halfway up the Atlantic coast between Florida and Maine. The bay is bordered by the states of New Jersey on the east and Delaware on the west. Fringed mainly by marshy lowlands, the bay also sports about 150 miles of beaches, some of which are lined with cottages and congested with vacationers in the summer. Delaware Bay is shallow and relatively warm, perfect for horseshoe crabs, which spend most of their year scuttling along the bay floor, hunting for worms and shellfish. Sandy beaches at the southern part of the Jersey shore, such as Reeds Beach, are prized by shorebirds because they slope gently to the water, where surf is not heavy. Also these beaches are but a short flight to roosting areas, such as Stone Harbor, along the Atlantic Ocean. Delaware Bay is a fragile ecosystem of global importance, all the more vulnerable because it is located near three huge U.S. cities—Washington, D.C., Baltimore, and Philadelphia.

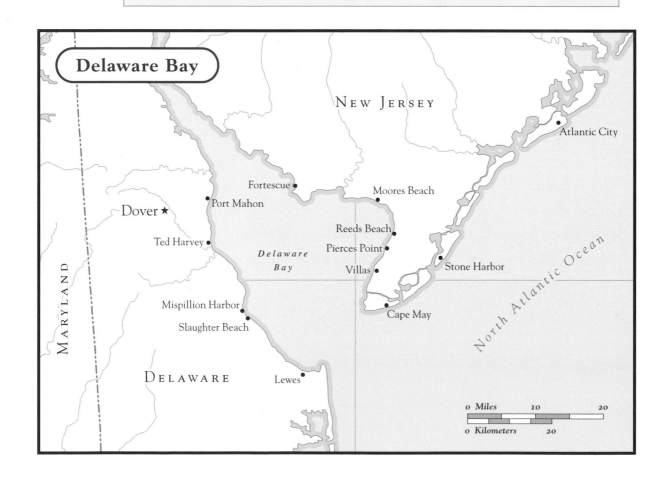

reproduce, so that *rufa* can survive. Over thousands of years, *rufa* red knots have some-how learned to synchronize their arrival at Delaware Bay precisely with the spring moons that draw the crabs from the water to deposit the great banquet of eggs in the sand. How migrating shorebirds made this discovery and developed such perfect timing is a mystery of science. How human biologists figured it out is, fortunately, much better known.

1979: A SPRINGTIME DILEMMA

For a long time shorebird experts had known that *rufa* red knots bred in the Arctic in June and July, and were aware that many of them wintered in South America. Two *rufa* stopover sites in Argentina had been mapped by the Belgian scientist Pierre Devilliers, and there were good leads to other South American sites soon to be explored.

The big mystery was, where did *rufa* go in the springtime? There were very few springtime knot references in birding literature, mainly reports from hunters who had observed flocks of knots flying overhead. Most biologists assumed the birds hopscotched their way up the Atlantic coast, stopping every few hundred miles. They agreed that a robin-sized bird could never make it from the bottom of the world to the top without stopping to refuel.

But where? In 1978 Brian Harrington, a shorebird biologist working for the Manomet Bird Observatory (now called the Manomet Center for Conservation Sciences), be-came determined to find out. He sent a form letter to about one hundred volunteer shorebird enthusiasts around the country. Harrington simply asked, "Does anyone know where there are more than 20–30 red knots in the spring?" Weeks went by with no response at all, until one afternoon Harrington picked up a phone call from a New Jersey man named Joe Lomacks.

"I got your letter," Lomacks said. "We have a lot of knots here on Delaware Bay in the spring."

"What do you mean by a lot?" asked Harrington. "Hundreds?"

"Thousands. At least thousands."

"Please send directions," Harrington replied.

During the last full week of May 1979, a skeptical Brian Harrington and his Mano-met colleague Linda Leddy drove from Massachusetts to New Jersey to check out Joe

Lomacks's story. The threesome met at a restaurant, piled into Lomacks's pickup, and drove south along the Jersey shore, finally pulling up behind a row of empty beach cottages at about 4:00 p.m. Harrington and Leddy climbed out and followed Lomacks down a puddle-strewn dirt road. Hardly anyone was around Reeds Beach—a tiny beachside cottage community a dozen miles north of Cape May—and wouldn't be until the Memorial Day vacation crowd arrived. The trio walked in silence until Lomacks cut between two houses, leading Harrington and Leddy onto the sand and up to the top of a beach ridge. Then he stopped.

On the beach before them were thousands and thousands of red knots, packed shoulder to shoulder. Many were jabbing furiously at some invisible food source buried in the sand. "You couldn't even see the beach," Linda Leddy recalled.

Brian Harrington struggled to contain his emotions. Here was a moment that few scientists experience, a single observation that changes all assumptions. "I was simply amazed," he recalls. "We had just published a paper—we scientists who thought we knew it all—saying there were only a few tens of thousands of red knots in the world, and here before us were at least that many knots on one little beach. Mr. Lomacks explained that they were eating the eggs of horseshoe crabs. It was news to me. There was nothing at all about a connection between shorebirds and horseshoe crabs in scientific literature. I had been picking up horseshoe crabs off beaches since I was a kid. But until that moment, I didn't have a clue about what they did for shorebirds."

THE ANCIENT GIVER

When tilting along a beach, the horseshoe crab (*Limulus polyphemus*) looks like a helmet dragging a barbed spear, leaving a road-grader-like print in the sand. More closely related to spiders and scorpions than to crabs, *Limulus* seems prehistoric, a living fossil, and it is. *Limulus* evolved 350 million years ago during the Permian geologic period, predating even the age of dinosaurs. The horseshoe crab is 50 million years older than birds, and many, many times older than humans.

Limulus spends most of its time on the ocean floor, foraging for invertebrates and worms. It lumbers ashore only to spawn under cover of night when a full moon signals the highest tide of the spring. By laying eggs at the highest tidal point, crabs ensure that

A multitude of shorebirds and gulls mass at Reeds Beach, 1983

subsequent high tides won't wash the eggs away before they get a chance to hatch. Though horseshoe crabs can be found in and around beaches from Maine to Mexico, the largest population by far resides in Delaware Bay, a huge inlet of the Atlantic Ocean that's relatively warm and shallow, and fringed with marsh creeks that provide good habitat.

Sand conditions at Delaware Bay are ideal for spawning crabs—compact enough to hold most eggs in place so that they won't wash away before hatching, yet porous enough to let oxygen penetrate down to the buried eggs. These ideal conditions led to a buildup of millions of horseshoe crabs at Delaware Bay over a long time. As recently as 1996, Brian Harrington calculated that if all the crab eggs at Delaware Bay were allowed to hatch and reach maturity, the crabs would cover 90 percent of the surface of New Jersey.

The horseshoe crab is what scientists call a "keystone" species, meaning one that is important to many other species, such as the shorebirds that turn crab eggs into fat in order to fly to their breeding grounds. For centuries, we humans have searched for ways

Starting in the mid-1800s, Delaware Bay fishermen captured huge quantities of horseshoe crabs and ground them up for fertilizer. This photo was taken in 1924

to make this slow-moving, easy-to-find creature important to us, too. Eating them, the most obvious idea, never worked well since there is very little meat on a horseshoe crab other than the muscle needed to move its arrowlike tail.

For a while we pulverized them. Starting in the mid-1800s, fishermen on both sides of Delaware Bay captured huge quantities of crabs, ground them into meal, and sold the meal to farmers to fertilize fields and feed chickens. More than 4 million crabs were killed in 1870 alone, when the stench of rotting crab corpses drew angry complaints from all around the bay. There are still places around Delaware Bay that mark the crab slaughter with names such as King Crab Landing and Slaughter Beach. Decade by decade, the *Limulus* population dwindled. It was rescued in the 1960s when it became cheaper for farmers to use new oil-based fertilizers than to pay fishermen to grind up crabs.

Limulus bounced back, and continued to serve our needs, though in unusual and unexpected ways. One way was as a research specimen. Starting in the 1930s, Dr. Haldan Keffer Hartline, a physiologist, performed experiments on the crab's enormous optic nerve to find out how *Limulus* managed to pick out shapes in dark, murky water. Dr. Hartline discovered that receptor cells in the crab's eye are interconnected, so that when one cell is stimulated, others nearby are depressed. This sharpens the contrast in light patterns. The breakthrough led to a clearer understanding of human vision, and a Nobel Prize in 1967 for Dr. Hartline.

There was an even greater gift to come. During the 1960s, the researchers Frederick Bang and Jack Levin discovered in *Limulus*'s blood a compound that protects the crabs against infection. They named the compound *Limulus* amoebocyte lysate (LAL). The scientists found that when crabs are exposed to germs, the LAL in their blood forms a clot around the infection, sealing it off and protecting the crab. By contrast, when human blood is infected, our immune system sends white blood cells charging out to fight the invaders. The LAL allows horseshoe crabs to withstand infection in frequently dirty water without an immune system to protect them.

Bang and Levin devised a simple test using *Limulus* blood to detect bacteria in medicines for humans. Exposing samples of medicines to LAL taken from the blood of a crab can quickly show whether or not medical equipment is infected, because a clot will form around an infection site. The LAL test works so well that the U.S. Food and Drug Administration now requires that every scalpel, drug, syringe, and flu vaccine be tested with LAL before being cleared for use on human patients. Gathering horseshoe crab blood has become a multimillion-dollar industry that depends on the blood of approximately 250,000 horseshoe crabs each year. As of this writing, a single quart of horseshoe crab blood can fetch $15,000 on the world market.

Medical testing, chicken feed, fertilizer—we humans

BLEEDING HORSESHOE CRABS AT A LYSATE FACILITY

Horseshoe crabs are collected by fishermen dragging the bottom of the ocean with nets. Once captured, crabs greater than eight inches across the widest portion of their shell are taken by truck to a lysate facility to be bled. In the room where the bleeding is performed, technicians wear gloves, coats, and hair nets to reduce the chance of bacterial contamination.

The crabs are mounted onto racks that bend the crab at the hinge region, exposing a quarter-size membrane into which a syringe needle is inserted. Approximately 30 percent of the crab's blood, about a coffee cup's worth, drains out into a collection bottle. The blood is blue—copper-based—rather than red like ours, which is iron-based.

The bottle of blood is placed into a centrifuge and spun to collect the white blood cells, called amoebocytes. The amoebocytes are converted into a yellowish liquid—the raw, precious, miraculous healing agent *Limulus* amoebocyte lysate (LAL).

When the operation is finished, the crabs are returned to the water. It takes about a week for the crab's blood volume to fill back up, but two to three months for blood counts to recover fully. The effect on crab populations is controversial. LAL industry spokespersons say that only about 3 percent of horseshoe crabs die during the operation, including harvest, transport, and return to the water. Other studies conducted by government agencies and universities put the figure as high as 30 percent.

never seem to run out of ideas for how this ancient ancestor can serve us. Horseshoe crabs seem indestructible, and it's true—no matter what we have demanded of them through the centuries, *Limulus* has always bounced back.

That is, until now. An idea born in the 1980s and reaching popularity a decade later threatens not only the horseshoe crab but the *rufa* red knot and other shorebirds as well. Here is a scene from a modern Delaware Bay drama:

CAPE MAY, NEW JERSEY, EARLY MORNING

Screaming gulls hover above the trawler. Below, a South Jersey fisherman brings an ax down heavily upon the shell of a horseshoe crab, smashing it in half and releasing a liquid with a pungent odor onto the deck. Two more swings and the creature is chopped into quarters. Guiding his vessel into the deeper waters of Delaware Bay, he cuts the motor and allows the boat to drift. He places several crab sections into a wooden pot and lowers it overboard with a strong line. Later in the day, he pulls up his pot and finds it filled with large twisted shells, the kind you put up to your ear to hear the ocean. Inside each shell is a snail known as a channeled whelk or, more popularly, a conch. That evening, he sells his harvest to a meat company.

A few weeks later, a shopper pulls a can of scungilli—or conch meat, as the label says—off the supermarket shelf and tosses it into her cart. Taking it home, she empties half the contents into a fresh green salad with sun-dried tomatoes, olives, and capers. She saves the rest to simmer later in marinara sauce. Or maybe she'll sprinkle it over pasta or risotto. She knows that any choice she makes, the taste of scungilli can be summed up in a single word: *heaven*.

Or the same fisherman might sell his whelk harvest to an exporter, who freezes the meat into blocks and ships it through the Panama Canal to Asia. Sliced paper thin, the Delaware Bay whelk, seduced into a bait pot by the fragrance of a slaughtered horseshoe crab, winds up in a Cantonese stir-fry dish offered on the menu of a Hong Kong restaurant. Still other fishermen chop up *Limulus* to bait American eels, also sold as delicacies to Asian food markets or used as bait to attract the even more lucrative striped bass.

•   •   •

Seemingly overnight, horseshoe crabs had become extremely valuable. They were like gold, and Delaware Bay had more than anywhere else. Tractor trailers with license plates from Massachusetts to Florida rumbled into small beach communities around Delaware Bay. Drivers hired local people to go to the beach, pick up crabs—especially the bigger, pregnant females—and toss them in the back. They drove away with heaping trailers and came back for more.

"The scale was unbelievable," recalls Larry Niles, then chief of the New Jersey Endangered and Nongame Species Program. "We didn't realize that there was this growing demand for horseshoe crabs all up and down the east coast. We were in a meeting one day when a colleague who had been doing crab surveys in the eighties got up and said, 'This year we counted only three hundred thousand crabs.' I was amazed. That was low—way low. Here we were so proud that we had these big concentrations of shorebirds around the bay, but it was all disappearing under our watch. If the crabs disappeared, so would the shorebirds. I knew in that moment that we had to do everything in our power to stop it from happening."

The pressure of a single decade's worth of bait fishing, combined with the use of horseshoe crabs for scientific research, now threatened to wipe out a 350-million-year-old species. Mature females, central to spawning, took the biggest hit. Because they released larger quantities of stronger-smelling liquid into the water when chopped up, they were the bait most prized. One survey by Virginia Tech University showed that the number of newly matured female crabs dropped by 86 percent between 2001 and 2003 alone. The statistic was all the more disturbing because each female crab took nine years to reach sexual maturity, when she would be able to reproduce.

At the same time, observers throughout the *rufa* red knot's hemispheric circuit were reporting drastically fewer birds. In the Arctic, scientists reported that nests had declined so dramatically that they were concerned that knots were having trouble finding one another to breed. Guy Morrison and Ken Ross, Canadian scientists who counted shorebirds each year from small airplanes flying at low altitudes over Tierra del Fuego, reported that half of the ninety thousand knots usually found at their key sites in Argentina and Chile had disappeared between 2000 and 2002. Some of their most reliable sites had no knots at all. A second dramatic population crash in 2007—possibly aggravated by a bloom of poison algae known as "red tide" along the coast of Uruguay—led Morrison and Ross to estimate that the entire South American wintering population had dwindled to fifteen thousand knots, a loss of 80 percent in a single decade. "I remember after one flight Ken and I got out of the plane and couldn't even speak," says Morrison. "We just looked at each other, like, 'Where are the birds?'"

Back at Delaware Bay, B95 sticks to his straightforward yet difficult task: find food, keep feeding, get ready to move on. With less food on the beaches now, there is little margin for error. Every day he has to lock down on an egg-laden beach quickly rather than wasting time and energy just flying around scouting for one. Every day, every tide, counts. The price of poor judgment is obvious: year by year, the flocks he flies with have become smaller and smaller.

B95 has to time the tides perfectly to take advantage of every bit of exposed shoreline during daylight hours. Ravenously hungry, he feeds from the moment he arrives at a beach to the minute the incoming tide bumps him over to the next beach or back to the roost.

B95, now in red breeding plumage, pushes through the days, the fat pouches beneath his skin filling steadily, adding muscle, transforming his body back into powerful flight-readiness for the final blast north. Each evening he flies with a large flock of knots to the communal roost on the ocean side of the Cape May peninsula to retire for a few hours of sleep.

In his memory, in his cells, through his hormonal system, in all the ways that *rufa* red knots understand things, B95 is determined that it isn't all going to end here at Delaware Bay. He has flown seven thousand miles in the past two months to reach this place, the greatest refueling station of all. Now he can sense it: he's almost there. He has but one last leg to go before he reaches his destination—the breeding grounds. Nothing will stop him. He is focused on finding a mate and raising at least one more brood of hatchlings.

The wind rises on the water and rustles the marsh grasses fringing the roost. A few birds chatter. B95 tucks his bill into his wing, closes one eye, and settles in for the night.

Brian Harrington in 1983, four
years after he first saw knots
at Reeds Beach

BRIAN HARRINGTON
Searching for Stepping-Stones

As a boy growing up in Rhode Island, Brian Harrington roamed the countryside with a BB gun, cheerfully picking off birds that strayed within his range. Late in the summer of his tenth year, a small flock landed in the farm field behind his house. He knew he had never seen birds anything like these, but he couldn't get close enough to inspect them, because the slightest motion sent them flashing away. Finally, one day he crawled on his belly close enough to squint at them through binoculars. They were about robin-sized, but stood taller on dark legs. They had swept-back wings with a crook at the elbow. Their jet-black faces were bordered with a thin margin of sugar white.

With the aid of a field guide, Brian discovered they were golden plovers, migratory shorebirds that each year flew an enormous loop between Alaska, where they bred, and South America, where they wintered. Their orbit was nine thousand miles long and two thousand miles wide. But no matter what, every August this flock returned to Brian's field as if magnetized. Something about the place was special to them. What was it? Brian traded his BB gun for a high-powered telescope and began to devote his life to understanding birds.

After college, Brian took a job with the Smithsonian Institution, banding seabirds on a small, isolated Pacific island named Johnson Atoll. The only spot of land for hundreds of miles around, it attracted multitudes of seabirds such as petrels, shearwaters, frigate birds, and terns during breeding season. Each evening Brian's crew would motor out to the island and band birds all night long. "We'd band until our fingers were sore," Brian recalls. "You'd just walk up to them and pick them up. They were awake, but dazzled by your headlight. I got so I could band five hundred birds in an hour."

Brian went back to Johnson Atoll the next year to see if any of his banded birds had returned. "The first night back I happened to walk up the same path I had used the year before. Right away I spotted a banded sooty tern and picked it up. The band around its leg had a number twelve on it. I picked up the bird next to it, and its band said number thirteen. The next bird was number fourteen. The birds were spaced out *exactly* as they had been the year before!"

It was an amazing example of nature's precision. After flying around much of the globe, these birds had returned to the same *square foot* of land. Why? What was so important about that place? How did they know where it was? Brian had been asking these questions since he first saw the plovers in the field behind his house, but the birds at Johnson Atoll suddenly fused his scattered thoughts into a single thesis. "I began to believe that certain beaches and flats and marshes where shorebirds gathered in the fall in New England were just like islands in the ocean are to seabirds," he later recalled. "They were critical places the birds need during a specific part of their lives, and from which they move on. These places were like stepping-stones in the migration systems of these birds. It also seemed that there aren't a lot of alternatives to those particular stepping-stones—the birds had to be *right there*. These places had to be conserved. And I was going to prove it."

Forty years later, Brian is still studying these questions as a shorebird scientist at the Manomet Center for Conservation Sciences. For most of these years, the *rufa* red knot has been the focus of his study. He has organized banding expeditions to Brazil and Argentina that have resulted in the discovery of some of *rufa*'s sacred stepping-stone places, such as Lagoa do Peixe. Some have been extremely difficult to reach. "We have hiked in mud to our knees, slept in leaking tents, and greeted scorpions in our shoes," he wrote.

But no single discovery has been more satisfying or important than the day in 1979 when Joe Lomacks led him to the multitude of knots at Reeds Beach. Here was the ultimate stepping-stone: a cluster of bay-shore beaches whose food supply attracted almost all *rufa* knots at the same time each year. As Brian Harrington puts it, "I had stumbled onto the strongest possible example of exactly what I was trying to prove."

Brian Harrington, at left, works with a young colleague in a nighttime catch

Chapter Four

TWINKLING AND TRAPPING

May 22, 2010: North Pierces Point Beach,
Delaware Bay, New Jersey

One touch of nature makes the whole world kin.   —Shakespeare

While B95 is fattening up on crab eggs to fuel his impending Arctic flight, a team of researchers, scientists, and students from all over the world converges on a single yellow cottage at Reeds Beach, on the Jersey side of Delaware Bay. Backpacks slung over their shoulders, hauling sleeping bags, air mattresses, laptop computers, spotting scopes, and other tools of their trade, workers from Australia, New Zealand, Britain, Taiwan, Quebec, Colombia, the United States, Argentina, Holland, and Spain tromp up the peeling steps and push through the screen door, noisily greeting one another. Several are here for the fourteenth year in a row to document and measure the activities of shorebirds and the horseshoe crabs whose eggs the birds depend on. Nine will sleep in the house, others in a nearby rented cottage, and still others in their trucks.

When the Delaware Bay Shorebird Project began in 1997, scientists simply sought to better understand the movements and requirements of shorebirds. But when it became all too clear that horseshoe crabs, red knots, and other shorebird species were struggling for their very existence, the focus widened to providing reliable scientific data to save these animals.

Having been invited to join the project, I am put to work instantly upon arrival. I am assigned to help two college students on the back porch string lime-green leg flags in numerical sequence onto a strand of wire. These are the flags that will be fitted around the legs of any birds we are lucky enough to capture. We all hope we'll get to band tomorrow. It will depend on the weather and if we can find a big enough flock and lure it within range of our cannon net.

The yellow cottage has the bustle of a fraternity house. Trucks and vans are parked on both sides of the puddle-pocked dirt road out front. The kitchen sink is piled high with dishes, and the living room is strewn with maps. A row of computer screens set up on a long table blazes at all hours as scientists tap in data. Graphs and tide charts and work assignment sheets are taped to the walls. On the back porch overlooking the bay, students sift through buckets of sand collected from several nearby beaches. Using tweezers to pluck horseshoe crab eggs from the sand, they set them aside so that they can compare the density of eggs with samples taken in previous years. As waves of a late-afternoon high tide lap against the porch standards below, there are probably a dozen studies of one kind or another taking place simultaneously within the walls of this small yellow cottage facing out onto the bay.

Today, May 22, is the midpoint of the spring knot migration to Delaware Bay. Knots have been pouring in night after night for about a week now, anticipating a feast of horseshoe crab eggs. There was a good crab spawn about a week ago, but since there are far fewer crabs than there used to be, it isn't clear whether they laid enough eggs in the sand to feed all the shorebirds. So far, it appears that most of the eggs have been deposited on three or four widely separated beaches near the mouths of creeks. The question of the day is: Will the shorebirds be able to find these beaches?

At 11:30 the screen door bangs shut behind Larry Niles. Niles is a solidly built man with a direct manner. He leaves no doubt who's in charge. Larry informs us that scouts have found a large mixed flock of red knots, ruddy turnstones, and sanderlings feeding at North Pierces Point Beach, several miles away. We're going to try to band them. High tide will occur at 2:00 p.m. We need to have the net ready on the beach at least an hour before.

I take my place in a sandwich assembly line, slapping mayonnaise onto bread slices

BANDING BIRDS

John James Audubon is believed to have been the first bird bander in North America. In 1803 Audubon tied a light silver thread around one leg on each of the birds he found in a nest at his father's farm. The next year, to his delight, the birds returned to the same nest. Today, several thousand federally licensed banders place rings around the legs of more than 1 million birds in the United States alone. The purpose of banding is to identify individual birds by marking them without hurting or overburdening them, so that their movements and habits and life histories can be studied. Success depends on resighting birds that have already been banded. For many years that meant recapturing banded birds, since identification numbers on metal bands were too small and faint to be seen even through telescopes. Today, laser-inscribed flags bearing large-print letter-and-number combinations (such as B95) can be seen through scopes. It is estimated that 10 to 15 percent of all living *rufa* red knots have been banded, perhaps the largest percentage of any shorebird.

as fast as I can. Others fill water containers, pack coolers, and stuff equipment into vehicles. Reaching our destination about noon, twenty-five of us spill out of cars and vans and haul our gear—a huge net, green tarps, reels of rope, iron tubes and projectiles for the cannons, and a detonator box, plus all our food and water—along a sandy path to a clearing in the marsh grass adjacent to a small, crescent-shaped beach.

Ten of us prepare the beach operation. First, the cannons: three holes are dug in the sand about forty feet apart at the top of the beach. A heavy iron tube, perhaps three feet in length, is lowered into each hole. A carefully measured amount of black powder is packed into each tube, followed by a long iron rod with a loop at the end to which the net will be attached. Dr. Clive Minton, the world's leading expert on cannon netting, carefully checks the elevation and angle of all three projectiles to make sure they match the wind and weather conditions. A long wire fuse sticking out of each cylinder is connected to the firing box, concealed in the grass.

Next, the net: our long, fine-mesh net is lowered in front of the three cannons and spread out onto the beach. It's red-colored and about the size of a tennis court. Six of us stand on the back line of rope, even with the cannons, and gather the mesh into our

Larry Niles, coleader of the Delaware Bay Shorebird Project, scans the beach as he prepares for a cannon netting

stomachs until all the slack is taken up. Now the net rests on the beach like a tightly rolled-up rug. We check to see that the front, or leading, rope is on top, so that it will unfurl in proper sequence when the cannon is fired and the projectiles pull the net out over the beach. Larry fastens ropes connecting the net to the projectiles. We camouflage the net by forcing it down into the sand and smoothing a thin layer over the top. A final layer of tidal wrack makes it look completely natural, at least to us. We hope the birds will agree.

At 12:30 we leave the beach and conceal ourselves behind a curtain of tall marsh grass. Now there's nothing to do but wait. High tide, when the birds will be pushed by advancing water into the smallest area possible, is still more than an hour away. Seated on folding beach chairs and atop plastic tubs of supplies, we smear on sunblock and try to keep quiet.

Larry rises to peer through binoculars out over the grass and onto the beach, which is bisected by a small creek opening into the ocean. There are flocks of shorebirds on both sides of the creek. We want the flocks to combine into one large flock on our side, so that the tide can push the birds in front of our net. Larry says there are maybe two hundred birds in all, but dispersed and scattered. I wonder: Is B95 among them?

Peter Fullargar and Mark Peck, team members who are deployed on the beach, communicate with Larry by walkie-talkie. All morning long Peter and Mark have been observing birds and radioing their position back. With the tide coming in steadily now, and the birds still separated by the creek, it's time to try to "twinkle" them together. *Twinkling* means getting close enough to shorebirds to be able to gently nudge a flock a short distance in one direction or another without spooking them into flight. Some people just have a knack for it. Peter and Mark are world-class twinklers.

Crackle of the radio:

Larry: "Start moving the birds toward us. Not a hard move. A twinkle. Come in real slow, just a little pressure. How many knots do you have? Over."

Peter: "About a hundred knots and a hundred fifty turnstones, twenty sanderlings. Over."

Under gentle pressure from the twinklers, the birds indeed start hopping over to our side of the creek, but only in groups of twos and threes. We need more for a good catch. Larry turns back to us, whispering that there are only a few birds within range and we may still have an hour to wait—if we even get a chance at all. I check one more time to make sure my cell phone is turned off.

Suddenly everything changes. For some reason, the birds are now crossing the creek in tens and twenties. The flocks have combined, and hundreds of shorebirds are feeding right in front of the net. "We're gonna go!" Larry hisses. Everyone rises to a sprinter's crouch. Dick Veitch, a stout, white-haired New Zealander, hovers over the firing box, finger poised. Gulls shriek overhead as we mentally review our specific jobs. Suddenly we hear Larry's rapid "Three, two, one," and then the cannons' muffled *boom!*

"Three, two, one," and then *boom!* A cannon net fires over a flock of shorebirds feeding on a Delaware Bay beach

We race through the rustling grass and burst out onto the open beach. The net is alive with struggling, chattering shorebirds. But its front edge has landed in the surf, and birds are trapped in the water. They will drown if we don't rescue them immediately. A half dozen of us plunge into the waves and, spacing ourselves evenly along the net, stretch our arms beneath the net and lift it as one, keeping our bodies low and driving the net forward onto the beach with our chests and thighs. As we work, others run to the back edge of the net, standing on it and weighing it down with heaps of sand so that birds trapped on the dry beach can't crawl out from under the net. Immediately we spread a dark green muslin tarp over the entire net, to shield the birds from sunlight and calm them with darkness.

Larry, Amanda Dey, and other experienced team members sink to their knees in wet sand and begin rolling the tarp back and untangling birds from the net. I run to fetch an empty box, and then return to the water, positioning myself behind workers who are freeing birds. We will keep separate boxes for red knots, ruddy turnstones, and

TRAPPING BIRDS

"When you're trapping animals of any kind there's a risk," says Dr. Amanda Dey, a shorebird expert and biologist with the New Jersey Endangered and Nongame Species Program. "But if you're going to find out what their lives are about, what their migration routes are, sometimes you have to lay your hands on them. When you do, you owe it to that animal to be as careful, as thoughtful, as quick to get them away and back to what they need to be doing as you can. Over many years, Clive Minton and Humphrey Sitters have worked out a protocol—a series of steps and rules—when cannon netting. Each step builds upon those before it. The aim is to minimize stress on the birds at every step of the way.

"I'm the animal rights person in the group. We do have mortalities—deaths. It happens. But it happens infrequently. I make sure that we brief everybody well before we trap birds. We go over how to hold a bird to cause the least stress. We review what everybody's job is and how to do it right so that accidents don't happen in the excitement. The data we've been able to get back helps to protect these birds. When I think about handling the birds, I ask myself again and again, 'Are you fair? Are you causing more harm than good?' I believe what we're doing is important and we need to keep doing it. But I have to say, every time I go cannon netting I have a knot in my stomach. If you don't, you shouldn't be doing this."

sanderlings. An untangler thrusts a bird in the air and yells, "Knot!"

"Knot!" I reply, meaning that I have a box for red knots.

I take the bird and deposit it gently through the opening in the top of the box. My box is lined with a green carpet on the bottom and has a Velcro flap over the slot on top. I continue to take knots until I have twelve. Then I carry the chattering, jiggling container to the top of the beach, where another worker transfers my knots into "keeping boxes," bigger, darker containers with better shade where they will stay until all the birds are free from the net. I return again and again to fill up boxes with birds. Because there are so many volunteers, the untangling and sorting of the entire catch—more than three hundred birds—takes only about half an hour.

Moments after a cannon shot, workers rush to disentangle birds trapped in the water

Now to collect the all-important data. We drag folding canvas chairs out onto the sand and arrange them in three adjacent circles. We organize into teams: one group will work with knots, one with turnstones, and one with sanderlings. Our job is to band, measure, and weigh each bird. Happily, I am assigned to weigh red knots. I will work with Amanda, known to all as Mandy, who will band them; Bill, who will measure with calipers the length of the bills and outer primary feathers; and Angela, Clive Minton's sister, who will draw a small sample of blood from the first thirty knots for testing to determine the gender of each. Christie will record statistics.

Everyone is on alert for B95. He has been spotted at Delaware Bay more than twenty times in the past but he has never been captured here. Several in our group have seen him. It is well known that he was observed just five months ago in Tierra del Fuego, so there is a good chance he is still alive and around here somewhere. Nothing would please the group more than to know that this legendary bird has reached Delaware Bay once again.

We peel off layers of clothing and pull ball caps down over our eyes to protect ourselves from a glaring sun in a spotless sky. Unexpected afternoon heat makes it even more important to take data quickly, to minimize the time the birds are held captive. Mandy starts our circle's operation by removing a knot from its keeping box and removing a plastic flag from the strand I strung yesterday. She gently wraps it around the knot's upper right leg and squeezes the ends together with pliers. Each lime-green band indicates that the banding took place in the United States, and is inscribed with a particular letter-and-number combination, such as A24. Mandy hands the bird to Bill, who performs his wing and bill measurements and then hands the bird to me.

A researcher examines a knot's feathers for wear

A researcher measures the length of a knot's bill. Males and females often have different bill lengths in relation to the size of their overall bodies

I place a digital scale onto a small table, then slide a cardboard tube into a cradle on top of the scale. My job is to place each bird inside the tube—briefly taking my hands away so that my weight isn't recorded—subtract the weight of the cradle, and call out the number that shows up on the digital readout.

I am amazed by the variation in weight in these birds. Some weigh almost twice as much as others. A few of my birds weigh only 90–100 grams (a little more than 3 ounces, since there are 28.34 grams to an ounce), while others weigh in the 180s. One butterball knot comes in at 190 grams. I can barely fit him in the tube. Most weigh in the 130–140-gram range.

Biologists estimate that a knot needs to weigh at least 180 grams when it leaves Delaware Bay in order to make it to the Arctic nonstop. That includes fuel left over in case the ground is still covered with winter snow in the bird's first days there. Since it is now May 22 and knots usually depart the Bay on or about May 28, that means my median-weight knots—those that weigh 130 grams—must gain about 8 grams per day before they leave. That's an increase of their body weight of about 6 percent each day. I would have to gain nearly 10 pounds a day to match that. Still, 8 grams per day is perfectly doable for a knot if there are enough horseshoe crab eggs on these beaches.

In 1997, the first year of the red knot study, about 80 percent of knots captured weighed at least 180 grams. The knot population on the bay that year was estimated at 50,000 birds. But over the last four years, only about 30 percent of the knots weighed 180 grams at the time of capture, and the estimated population reaching Delaware Bay is now only about 14,475 birds. By documenting the decline in both numbers and weight, scientists hope to support a bid to protect *rufa* red knots under state and federal endangered-species laws, and also to build a case to protect key stopover sites throughout the hemisphere.

The presence of a number of birds on my scale in the 180–190-gram range is a hopeful sign. It shows that some have been able to find enough food on the beaches. The smaller birds in the 120-gram range have probably just arrived from South America. When I draw my finger along the feathers in the breasts of these birds, I can feel their

FRANK "THUMPER" EICHERLY: A DELAWARE BAY WATERMAN

Frank Eicherly, known to all as "Thumper," is a fifty-two-year-old fisherman from Frederica, Delaware. He owns a fifty-foot-long trawler named *Maggie S. Meyers*, outfitted with rakes connected to chains that drag behind the boat and "dredge" sea creatures off the bottom of the bay and into a bag. "I call it the 'tractor of the sea,'" Thumper says.

Thumper started dredging in the bay as a young man. Until the last decade or so, he dredged up hundreds of crabs each outing, selling them to bait fishermen and meat exporters from all over the world. But much changed a few years ago, when awareness of the link between shorebirds and horseshoe crabs, and of declining populations of each, came to light. Regulations designed to protect the crabs and shorebirds placed tight restrictions on crab harvesting in Delaware waters. "Since all these changes, I can't make a living on the water," Thumper says.

"Yes, I have seen people exploit the horseshoe crab," he says, "but I think the trouble was with people taking them off beaches, loading them in trailers, and driving away. And now we watermen are paying the price."

He adds, "You have to admire red knots. They look like delicate little rascals, but that's one heck of a trip they fly. It's more than just an ocean. It's the whole hemisphere. And they're out there in the wind and rain. I just hope a way can be found to rebuild the crab population so everyone—knots, crabs, and watermen—can survive."

sharp breastbones poking just beneath the skin. These lighter knots will have to feed steadily, for they have arrived late and are behind the others. They have a lot of weight to gain and not much time. They will need to gulp down big quantities of horseshoe crab eggs—*if* they can find them. Recently some birds have taken to sticking around Delaware Bay an extra week, until June 3 or 4, to take on more fuel. That is a risky strategy, for if they arrive too late in the Arctic, mates and breeding territories may be taken.

One hopeful sign is that a full moon next week will bring a second spring tide, ideal conditions for spawning horseshoe crabs. Some years there are two spring tides while the birds are here, sometimes only one. We've already had one. With luck and good weather, there could be one more big batch of horseshoe crab eggs to help the tardy knot arrivals gain enough weight to fuel their two-thousand-mile Arctic flight.

Now, as we pass the knots from hand to hand, some squeal and wriggle. A few beat their wings frantically and resist my effort to stuff them into the weighing tube. One spins out of my grasp, drops to the sand, and flutters away. Yet many birds are quiet and passive. It's a huge responsibility to handle these birds, for clearly we are placing them under stress. Being captured forces them to burn precious energy and removes them from a feeding cycle. Some birds fly away when released, but most wobble off on foot.

When the last bird is released, we stand up and stretch. Our muscles remind us we've been sitting in a cramped position for nearly four hours. In all, it was a magnificent catch. More than three hundred birds were banded and examined. Thirty were recaptured birds, meaning they had already been banded. Three birds had orange Argentine bands when they reached my weighing station today—causing my pulse to quicken—but none turned out to be B95.

Later, back at the yellow house at Reeds Beach, over pasta and salad the conversation turns to B95. It's already May 22 and no one has reported him yet. We wonder: Is he just arriving tonight from South America, way behind schedule, bony and starving at 100 grams? Or is he already fat and confident from having been here a week or more? Maybe he's practicing his breeding display flights and mating calls, just as he will in the Arctic.

Someone yawns and checks his watch. It's late. Chairs are scraped back and cups

B95 AT DELAWARE BAY

According to the Web site www.bandedbirds.org, B95 was spotted twenty-three times on several beaches around Delaware Bay between 2005, when the database was established, and 2009. Except for once, he was always observed between May 17 and May 25, with May 19 being the most frequent date—six spottings. This shows he usually arrives early enough to gain the weight he needs.

B95 has never been captured at Delaware Bay—all the reports came from observers who spotted his orange band and distinctive letter-and-number combination through binoculars or spotting scopes. With his fame growing year by year, everyone is eager to catch a glimpse of him.

When the Argentine researcher Luis Benegas saw him in the rain at Moores Beach on Delaware Bay in 2009, he called it "the happiest day of my life."

rinsed in the sink. Larry Niles reads aloud the tide table taped to the wall and lines out tomorrow's work schedule for those who will be scouting the beaches. Now it's time to tromp upstairs and squirm into a sleeping bag. We can pick up our discussion tomorrow. For now, all of us in the yellow cottage who shared this exciting day of field science can only hope that B95 is, like us, somewhere safe and comfortable as the night hurries by.

Chapter Five

THE ARCTIC BREEDING GROUNDS

June and July: Central Canadian Arctic

I came to think of the migrations as breath, as the land breathing. In spring a great inhalation of light and animals. The long bated breath of summer. And an exhalation that propelled them all south in the fall. —Barry Lopez, from *Arctic Dreams*

The only way for us to know for sure whether B95 has made it safely from Delaware Bay to the Arctic Circle this year is for someone to spot him after his breeding time ends and he and other red knots stream back south to a stopover site. Trying to discover the few acres of his personal mating territory within the entire red knot breeding grounds—an area bigger than Alaska—would be nearly impossible. So there is nothing to do now but wait, and hope.

FLEDGLING DAYS

Like all *rufa* red knots, B95 was born in the pale light of endless summer, deep within northern Canada. His birth year was most likely in the early 1990s, though it could have been earlier. He was probably one of four hatchlings, a typical number for red knots, having poked his way out of an egg that had been leaning against three

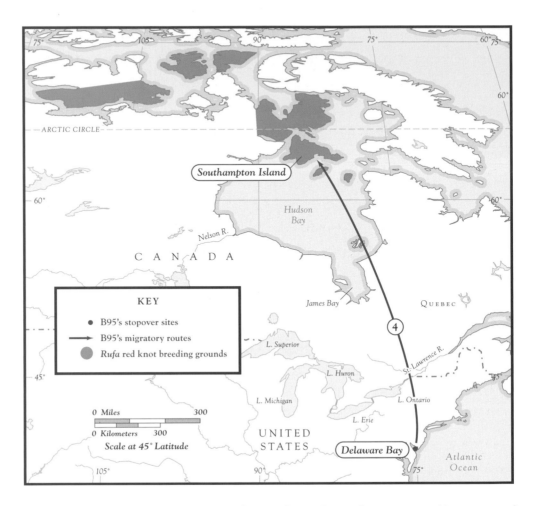

others in a shallow, moss-lined scrape in the earth. B95's mother gave up 60 percent of her body weight when she released those four precious eggs into the scrape.

B95's parents had arrived in northern Canada in the early part of June after three months and nine thousand miles of flying, refueling, and moving on. Though their plumage was fresh brilliant red, the barbs of their flight feathers were ragged and frayed from millions and millions of strokes. B95's parents had likely been mates in years before, and had managed to find each other once again. Perhaps his mother had recognized mating calls his father had uttered while they were still at Delaware Bay. Probably they traveled north together in the same flock, and when the flock dispersed to spread out over the vast breeding grounds of the lower and central Arctic, the couple stayed together.

The landscape in this part of the Arctic tundra is a vast desert of bleached rocks and wiry grass, riddled by shallow ponds that are often icebound when the knots arrive. Except when an animal crunches its way over the snow or cries out, or when ice cracks like a rifle shot, the only sound is the howling, moaning, whistling wind. The long days of Arctic summer are bathed in light. When the sun reaches its highest point, even the rocks blaze white. When it sinks to low angles near the horizon on a clear day, everything from the smallest seed head of a plant to the breast of a red knot glows in warm red light as if lit by a torch.

If B95's birth year was typical, his parents had little to eat during their first few days in northern Canada. Deep snow still banked against cobblestone ridges and blanketed much of the land, though bare patches of earth appeared and widened under the melting heat of a sun that hung low in the sky almost all day long. The knots survived by burning leftover horseshoe crab fat from Delaware Bay and by scavenging saxifrage buds and last season's crowberries from the ground.

And then, as the summer days lengthened, the sun finally unlocked the bounty they had flown all the way from Argentina for: bugs! Millions and millions of insects. Most were mosquitoes that had been living under the snow during the winter, relying on a chemical in their bodies to keep them from freezing. When the ice melted and the ground at last became spongy, they were freed. They bred almost instantly in the still pools, producing a blossom of protein-rich larvae—even more knot food. Stiff, punishing winds pinned the bugs down close to the ground within easy reach of the ravenous knots, who snatched them up on the pond margins. Soon the deeper lakes melted, releasing a second bloom of protein. Spiders hatched in the mossy uplands. Now the earth was fragrant and the tundra swarmed with insects and food was everywhere!

B95's soon-to-be father got right to work. He staked

GETTING READY TO REPRODUCE

Knots transform themselves yet again to get ready for breeding activity. Some males develop a sex urge before they reach the Arctic. They start practicing display flights and mating calls even at Delaware Bay. But they can't act on these urges. To save weight during flight, males do not develop their sex organs until they reach the breeding grounds. Females make even greater changes. The four eggs they will deposit consist mainly of calcium, but there is very little calcium in the insect food they will eat in the Arctic. So they eat as much calcium as they can *before* departing for the Arctic, storing it mainly in their legs. They fly this egg-making material into the breeding grounds, but they can't carry too much or else they'll burden themselves down as they fly. They have to get it just right. Scientists estimate that female knots import into the Arctic about one-third of the calcium they need.

A male red knot displays his showiest dance moves to attract a mate during courtship

out a patch of tundra as his breeding territory. To a human observer, there wouldn't be a thing about this spot that made it stand out, but he knew every rock, ridge, tussock, and puddle within it; it was a sacred slice of the earth he would give his life to defend.

He then took to the sky to advertise his fitness as a mate. He began by pumping himself nearly five hundred feet into the air on stiff, quivering wings. Reaching his peak, he lifted his wings above his shoulders and slanted downward, singing three sharp syllables over and over. Just before he hit the ground, he tucked into a horizontal glide and switched his call to a different, two-note melody. Finally, with his wingtips pointed downward and quivering rapidly, he pumped himself back up high over the tundra and glided to the ground to stand with outstretched wings near his chosen mate.

B95's father found a spot concealed within lichen-covered rocks and tussocks of grass, and scraped out a hollow in the earth. He and his mate lined it with moss and leaves. A few days later there were four eggs in the scrape. For the next three weeks the couple shared parenting duties, taking turns sitting on the eggs all day and night to keep them warm.

Then, about three weeks later, in the early part of July, B95 pecked and poked and wriggled his way out of his shell. Though wobbly at first, he could do most of what he needed to do within hours. He could walk, hunt, and use his wondrous black bill to feed himself before he was even a day old. He had no flight feathers as yet, but a coat of soft down covered his body and kept him warm. Hours after he hatched, he and his fellow nestlings abandoned their scrape in the earth and walked with their parents across the tundra to the margin of a pond, where they joined other shorebirds that were feeding on insects.

STUDYING KNOTS IN THE ARCTIC

"Knots are among the most difficult Arctic species to survey," writes biologist Larry Niles. "We have walked within three feet of a nest and the incubating knot just sat tight. Most shorebirds flush at greater distances."

In 2001, Niles became the first researcher ever to find an active red knot nesting territory. He did so by attaching radio transmitters to a few knots when they were in Delaware Bay and following them to the Arctic. Once there, he chartered a bush plane that swept back and forth over the featureless breeding grounds in a grid pattern, while Niles listened intently through headphones for a radio signal. When he finally heard the first faint beeps, he knew he was in luck at last. The birds had established breeding territories on Southampton Island near the entrance of Hudson Bay. The nests were spread far and wide—sometimes fewer than two per square mile—making them very hard to find.

Biologists working in the Arctic during mosquito season must ensure that their skin is protected

(LEFT) Four knot eggs blend in with the tundra vegetation, making them hard for predators to spot
(ABOVE) A soon-to-be parent keeps the eggs warm

Nature had put B95 on a fast track toward independence. He had to grow up quickly, for just a few days after he was hatched his mother flew away, spiraling up and off into the pale sky with the other adult females.

The fathers and other adult males stayed behind to keep the young birds safe and warm at night and protect them from predators. Danger was all around. Gull-like jaegers hovered over the tundra, scanning for shorebird eggs and chicks to snatch up. Stealthy white arctic foxes and snowy owls were always near. B95 quickly learned that his father's sharp cry meant to freeze *right where you were*. He was not yet able to fly, so his only defense was to remain absolutely motionless and rely on his mottled plumage to blend in with grasses and rocks. When a fox approached too closely, advancing and sniffing and finally raising a foot to pounce, B95's father would explode into flight, giving a sharp warning call. Often a predator would fall for it—chasing the parent instead of the newborns, only to be left without any prey as the adult bird veered away to safety at the last minute.

B95 grew very rapidly. His downy coat soon gave way to his first feathers, brownish gray with white edging. His black legs muted into a yellowish color. He was always hungry. Because it never got completely dark, he could spend all day poking around the shorelines and seeps for larvae, sometimes wandering back up a hill for the spiders that seemed to crawl over every tuft of grass. There were beetles and cutworm larvae. But even if there were no insects, an adaptable knot could get by on sedge seeds, horsetails, and grass shoots.

B95's bill was still not developed enough to jab for food, so he scooped his prey off the surface of the pond margins. He tested his new wing feathers with flights that were short and wobbly at first, but which steadily increased in altitude, velocity, and length. He learned to bank and tack into the tundra gales that whistled across the landscape. And then one day, when the wind rose and a slight chill entered the air, B95's father disappeared, too, winging away with the other adult males.

Now B95 and the other young birds, not yet a month old, were on their own. They fed steadily, getting heavier and stronger, working their flight feathers, learning to read danger without the protection of adults. They remained on the tundra until the day, early in August, when an urge to leave seized them. It was not a thought, not an idea, but a powerful restlessness that took over all the young birds on the breeding grounds of the barren Arctic. Summer was slipping away. It was time to go.

B95's fledgling days were finished. His flight feathers were well developed now, ready for a serious test, one that would challenge his ability to survive. B95, the great athlete who would become known to humans as the most successful of all *rufa* red knots, was poised to begin the first of his many marathon flights. One day, in the company of the other young knots, he lifted his wings and rose up to begin a life on the wind.

This arctic fox, whose silky fur blends in with the snowscape, is a deadly predator of young shorebirds

Amanda Dey with one of her favorite shorebirds, the American oystercatcher

AMANDA DEY
Migratory Bird Biologist

Dr. Amanda Dey, principal zoologist for the New Jersey Endangered and Nongame Species Program, has been studying red knots throughout their hemispheric circuit since 2001. She is an ecologist with special expertise on migratory birds. She oversees the Delaware Bay Shorebird Management Plan and is working to refine a Web-based system for people to report sightings of marked shorebirds. She maps landscapes where shorebirds are found and, with teammates, is building a way to track the movements of migratory shorebirds throughout the western hemisphere.

"I wanted to be a wildlife biologist all my life," Dey says. "I got my start down by the railroad tracks, looking for tadpoles in drainage ditches. My mom was always pointing out the birds to me. Our family had a house down at the Jersey shore, and I spent many happy hours seining things like crabs and seahorses and blowfish from the bay. I loved being outdoors."

But after high school, Dey hesitated to pursue her dream of being a biologist. Paralyzed by doubt about whether she could handle college math and science courses, she worked as a secretary. Self-confidence finally arrived when she was twenty-seven. "I just went for it," she says. "I enrolled in college and took all the math and science courses they had from beginning algebra to calculus. Now I use it all the time: algebra for problem solving, statistics to read graphs and understand how data are distributed. And school gives you research skills."

Dey and her husband, Larry Niles, have followed *rufa* red knots throughout their annual migratory circuit. She has a special love for the Arctic. "It's like a desert," she says. "It's quiet and stark and beautiful. But you must constantly remember that you're not in control there. Polar bears rule. They're the top of the food chain. For years we saw only tracks, but then one year we had six bears coming off the ice early and migrating up a ridge near our tents. They're stealth predators. You have to remind yourself to turn around every once in a while and look for them when you're hiking. If you get threatened, you start by firing off firecrackers and hope that scares them away."

For the past several years Dey and Niles have researched breeding knots in the Canadian Arctic. The area they've studied the longest, a plot of ten hectares (about twenty-five acres) on Southampton Island, has offered discouraging news. "The first year there were ten nests within our study area," she says. "Now it's down to one or two. In 2005 there were none at all."

Why study knots? "Knots are fascinating," Dey says. "They're like a really exclusive clique. They hang around in tight groups. They travel together. Besides, shorebirds are underdogs. You have to be a voice for wildlife and stand up for them. I'm inspired by the goodwill of all the researchers and volunteers at Delaware Bay. People around the world are trying to help these birds. I tell you, if you hold a shorebird in your hands only one time, you are changed forever. You'll come back year after year. These birds need all the help they can get. And I am determined to help them."

Chapter Six

MINGAN:
THE BELLWETHER SITE

July and August: Mingan Archipelago, Quebec, Canada

A journey of a thousand miles begins with a single step.

—Lao-tzu, Chinese philosopher (604–531 BC)

On the chilly morning of August 25, 2008, a young French biologist named Cédrik Juillet saw several dozen red knots drop onto a tidal flat around Niapiskau, an island in the Mingan Archipelago of eastern Quebec. Instantly they began to feed. Juillet snapped into his time-tested mode of sneaking up on birds. He advanced five steps, froze, squinted through his scope, scribbled down what he saw, and advanced five steps more. Using this method, Juillet got so close that when he tightened the lens of his telescope the last time, he could read the letter-and-number code combinations on the legs of knots that had been banded.

This little flock was a miniature United Nations! It contained birds from all over the western hemisphere. One wore the lime-green flag indicating it had first been banded in the United States, and another the blue Brazilian flag. Scanning slowly from left to right, Juillet picked out the red of Chile, and the familiar yellow flag of Canada. Then he spotted a bird sporting the orange flag of Argentina on its upper left leg and a *black* band on its lower right leg. *Black?* Where was that from?

A few hours later Juillet joined other researchers to compile the day's data. "I saw a bird with a black band today," he said to nobody in particular. "What's up with that?" Yves Aubry, an ornithologist for the Canadian Wildlife Service and the project leader, pushed his chair back and turned toward him. "Does the flag say B95?" Juillet ran his finger to mid-page in his notebook and stopped. There it was: black band, orange flag, B95. "How did you know that?" Juillet asked him.

Aubry produced a photograph taken in Argentina by the biologist Patricia González of the same bird in Tierra del Fuego, half a world away. González had urged Aubry to keep an eye out for this incredibly old, amazingly successful knot who was becoming a hero in Argentina. They had a special name for him: "Moonbird."

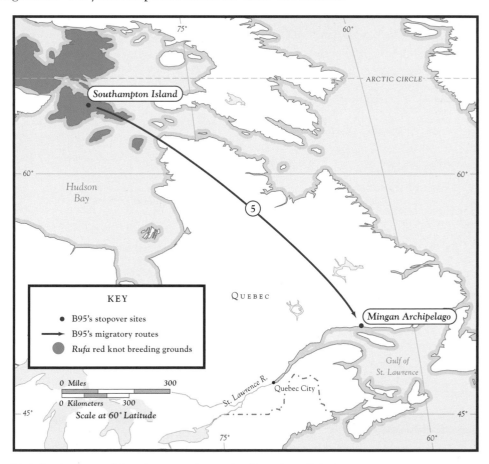

B95's first journey, and that of many newborn *rufa* red knots, is a flight between the breeding grounds of the Canadian Arctic and the Mingan Archipelago at the mouth of the St. Lawrence River in northern Quebec, Canada

THE MINGAN ARCHIPELAGO

Along the north shore of the Gulf of St. Lawrence, in Canada's province of Quebec, is a collection of some forty islands and more than a thousand islets and reefs known as the Mingan Archipelago. This amazing place became a Canadian national park in 1984.

Most of the islands were fashioned from very soft bedrock called limestone. Over thousands of years, powerful tides have sculpted channels into the limestone and separated the material into islands. But the water didn't stop there. It kept right on sculpting. Today there are approximately two thousand weirdly beautiful objects that stand alone on the shorelines of the Mingan Islands. Called "monoliths," they look to some like objects of pottery, or even like giant game pieces that have been dropped onto the beaches from above. Some are covered with plants, others are bare.

There are many wild plants and animals at Mingan. It is a wonderful place to search for seals and dolphins. Whales are attracted to shoals of plankton in the cold waters of the Gulf of St. Lawrence. Seabirds such as puffins gather in colonies. And, of course, red knots flock to Mingan in summer and early autumn.

This was not the first time B95 had excited researchers with his presence at Mingan. In fact, every year since 2006, when Yves Aubry first assembled a research team to study shorebirds arriving at the islands in late summer, B95 has been among the red knots present. Headquarters is a two-story white house in Mingan Village with windows facing out upon the Mingan River. Early each morning, sleepy-eyed researchers pack lunches, grab their spotting scopes and notebooks, pull on their muddy boots, and duck under a clothesline sagging with yellow rain slickers, safety vests, and wet wool jackets as they make their way out of the house and into the clean, salty air.

Local fishermen are already hard after crabs, scallops, periwinkles, and lobsters. The biologists drive to a dock at Mingan's harbor, often pausing for a moment to watch minke whales frolic in the channel. They lower themselves into a small boat whose driver ferries them to the islands they will be surveying for birds that day. He will pick them up again in the afternoon for data-entering sessions back at the house.

The Mingan Archipelago has a special importance among *rufa*'s stepping-stone sites. Mingan is the bellwether site—the first indicator of trends. The knots that fly into

THE MYSTERY OF THE MISSING KNOTS

In 1996 there were an estimated 150,000 knots leaving Delaware Bay to fly north to breed in the Arctic in spring (now there are many fewer). But shorebird surveyors were counting only 50,000 knots returning from the Arctic in the fall. Where were the 100,000 missing knots? Experts had long believed that, after breeding, nearly all *rufa* knots returned south through central Canada, and then flew on to beaches and marshes along the east coast of the United States before blasting to South America.

But the numbers didn't add up. Manomet's Brian Harrington wondered if there was an undiscovered stepping-stone "somewhere north of the United States [from which] they fly directly to South America."

In 2006 scientists began to suspect that the Mingan Archipelago could provide at least part of the answer after Yves Aubry of the Canadian Wildlife Service reported hundreds of red knots feeding on the tidal flats of Mingan's westernmost islands. On July 19 of that year Aubry and two colleagues, Sebastien Paradis and Yann Troutet, counted nearly a thousand knots on the island of Niapiskau alone. Week after week, island by island, knots kept pouring in.

Aubry reported this finding to other shorebird biologists in Canada and the United States. "At first they didn't believe us," Aubry recalls. "But then several came up to visit, and seeing was believing."

Mingan offer the year's first clue as to whether the *rufa* breeding season has been a success, a disaster, or something in between. An early sign that things have gone wrong in the Arctic is a first wave that contains a near-equal mixture of males and females. "That's not a good sign," says the University of Toronto's Dr. Allan Baker. "The first wave should be females, arriving a long time before the males."

Scientists pay special attention to juvenile birds. They hope that at least 20 percent of the three incoming waves combined are young birds. Few young birds arrived in 2006 and 2007, the first two years of intensive study, but in 2008, a large group of juveniles scattered over the islands just weeks after their mothers, and then their fathers, had arrived—an encouraging sign.

A FLEDGLING'S FIRST JOURNEY

B95 had surely been to the Mingan Archipelago many times before he was spotted by researchers. In fact, B95's very first migratory flight, when he left the Arctic with a flock of month-old birds, was almost certainly a 1,500-mile nonstop odyssey from the central Arctic to the Mingan Archipelago.

Though we don't know the exact route B95 took to Mingan on that flight, the most direct route would have drawn the young flock on a southeasterly course over the northern part of Canada's Hudson Bay. We can imagine that the knots flew over open water for several hours until they heard the pounding of surf against a shoreline and the air shook with thermal updrafts of warmer air rising from their first landform—the rugged coast of Quebec. For many hours they continued over land, shadowing bare rocky hills whose valleys were veined with green shrubs. Herds of caribou strung out in long trains below them, visible on a clear day, often in the company of the darker, smaller outlines of wolves packed tightly together.

Still fat with fuel from the mosquito protein they had devoured in the Arctic, they sliced through the air with little fatigue in the beginning hours of the journey. B95 surely called out to his flock mates, and they would have called out, too, maintaining a moving, opinionated web of contact. Though the young birds had never flown through this air or above this land before, the flock moved tightly together, each bird relying on impulses and directional signals from an internal guidance system, but also gaining information from the flock itself.

Morning light would have revealed a changed landscape over southern Quebec, a carpet of pointed green trees, pitted with lakes and bogs. Perhaps moose raised their heads, water streaming from beards and antlers, at the sound of the chattering birds above. And something else probably changed: after nearly two days of constant work without food, flight was surely no longer an effortless reflex for B95. Now it must have been a struggle that required all his concentration and strength. Panting rapidly through a parted bill, B95 pulled all the oxygen he could from the air to satisfy his burning lungs—and kept on stroking. Perhaps some of his companions slowed, and faltered, and fell as the flock moved on.

When at last the wide St. Lawrence River appeared in the distance, with the Atlantic Ocean glimmering on the left, B95, starving and exhausted, entered a long, tapering descent that ended when he raised his wings one last time and pitched to a stop on an island shore.

FAST LEARNER

You think you have to learn a lot? Consider B95. Brian Harrington has ideas about why this one phenomenal bird has lived such a long and successful life. To Harrington, it boils down to learning.

"Think about it. Say B95 stopped at Mingan on his first southward migration. When he got there he had to find enough food to fly over the ocean to South America without stopping so he could get to South America in time to molt on their wintering grounds.

"So B95 arrives at Mingan. He's three months old and he's from the Arctic, and he's never been where the water comes in and covers up everything two times a day. He's never eaten a marine invertebrate. He has to figure out how to use this whole tidal system. He has to learn that two hours after high tide you can go to a certain tidal flat, because it's the first to get exposed and it has some good clams in it.

"Then an hour and a half later he has to know he can fly another four hundred yards up the bay to find this next tidal flat that has some good mussel spat in it, and then two hours after that you can go to the next tidal flat. Some birds put all that together, and when the time and weather are right, they're ready. Others don't, but they go anyway and don't make it. B95 has learned how all these systems work and faced all the new kinds of predators. And then he goes to southern Brazil and has to learn it all over again, and then in the winter grounds learn it all over again. The challenges to survival are *huge*, as is the opportunity to mess up in any one of these places. So in any given year, more and more of the mates he hatched with in the Arctic are gone. But B95 has done everything right. B95 is a brilliant bird."

FIRST DAYS AT MINGAN

If the year of B95's birth was typical, his parents had already been at Mingan for weeks. His mother arrived first in early summer, flying with other females, many of them like her, amazing athletes that had somehow found the energy to migrate less than a month after having deposited more than *half* their body weight in the form of four eggs. Their head start to Mingan gave them the first chance for food free of competition from males and juveniles. Next came the males, most of them fathers that had stayed behind to raise the chicks. B95 arrived in the last wave, with the other young birds. For knots, Mingan is like a major international airport: the timing of arrivals and departures of *rufa* waves is so precise that by the time B95 touched down at Mingan, his mother may have already left for points south.

As always, food was the main attraction at

After regrowing his gizzard, B95 could grind up food such as the periwinkle snails on this seaweed

A juvenile red knot, only a few weeks old, newly arrived at Mingan. Note the yellowish legs, a sign of a young bird

HERBST CORPUSCLES AND THE WONDROUS KNOT BILL

B95 doesn't just poke around randomly in the sand or mud for food. His feeding is much more precise than that, thanks to a wonderful feature in his bill. The very tip of a knot's bill has a cluster of nerve receptors called Herbst corpuscles, which sense changes in pressure. When the birds jab their bills in and out of wet sand in the same spot, they create pressure in the seawater surrounding the sand particles. If a hard object like a clam is nearby, the Herbst corpuscles detect a disturbance in this pressure, giving away the object's presence. This sensory capability leaves the prey with nowhere to hide. So, in a way, B95 feeds by touch.

Mingan for B95 and his mates. The Mingan specialty is the mussel *Mytilus edulis*, which clings by a strong thread to rocks on the island shores. Its blue shell is easy to see when the tide is out during daylight hours. Mingan's menu also features shrimp, snails, and clams for the taking.

B95 soon discovered in his first days at Mingan that shelled animals were too hard to grind up. He had eaten only soft food back in the Arctic—mostly insects. In fact, his bill had just recently grown long enough to poke for food in the mud; for most of the summer he had to scoop his prey off the surface of the ground.

But knots are masters of transformation. They seem to be able to change their bodies to do anything they need to do. During his first few days at Mingan, B95 got by on insects—soft food—while he *grew* an organ to grind up the shelled prey he coveted. To save weight during his flight to Mingan, his gizzard, as the grinding organ is called, had remained small and light. But now he needed it. By day four, he had completely regrown it. From then on, there was hardly a shelled creature at Mingan safe from the attack of this confident young predator.

MISSING

Because B95 has been observed at Mingan every year since the research program began in 2006, his legend has spread throughout French Canada. When B95 appeared in 2009, a Montreal newspaper sent a reporter to Mingan to write a story about him, naming him Bob, after the "B" on his flag. The journalist even turned it into a love story, giving him a mate, Bobbette. Quebec schoolteachers began organizing units around the amazing bird who spent a few weeks in Quebec each summer, asking students to map the route of the Moonbird and estimate the distance he had flown. An animated feature for students featuring B95 went into production.

But as the weeks of summer 2010 passed, researchers and volunteers alike became worried that B95 had not appeared at Mingan. A large flock of female birds arrived on time at Mingan in mid-July, followed a month later by a fine showing of males. Late in August the first juveniles appeared; more kept pouring in day after day until their numbers built to nearly three hundred by late September. Spirits were high. Encouraging signs pointed to a productive breeding season. But where was B95?

A cannon netting captured 112 males on August 13. All but two birds caught in the net were males, pointing to breeding success—these were the dads that stayed behind. But concern spread that the great old knot, B95, was missing from the catch. This would have been the best chance of all to capture him, within a large group of males. Everyone was aware that he had not been seen anywhere in the world since December 2009 in Tierra del Fuego. The question hung unspoken in the air: Had B95 met his end at last?

Six days later, Yves Aubry, working alone in the early-afternoon hours of a windless day, came upon a group of eight knots feeding on the flats of Quarry Island. Aubry could tiptoe close enough to tell that most had adult plumage, but he couldn't quite see if they were banded. They kept moving. He kept moving. And then, for a long moment, they settled in one spot. Aubry tightened the focus in his eyepiece.

B95 AT MINGAN

July 29, 2006. At Niapiskau Island. Probably failed to breed, based on his early arrival date. Successful male breeders usually begin to arrive August 5–10.

August 25–26, 2007. At Quarry Island. Probably bred.

August 25, 2008. At Niapiskau Island. Probably bred.

August 14, 2009. At Niapiskau Island. Probably bred.

August 19, 2010. At Quarry Island. Probably bred.

Yves Aubry at Mingan

At 3:23 p.m. the conservationist Julie Valcourt from Parks Canada received a static-filled radio message from somewhere far out on Quarry Island. Through the breaks and crackles, she managed to scribble down Aubry's agitated words and relay them as instructed in French to Dr. Allan Baker in Toronto, who at 4:51 passed the message in English on to Dr. Charles Duncan of the Manomet Center for Conservation Sciences. Dr. Duncan immediately sent an e-mail bouncing off a communications satellite and down into laptops, desktops, and smartphones around the world. Dr. Duncan's message was short but triumphant: "B95 is alive!"

"The great thing was that he showed up late in the summer," Yves Aubry later said from his office in Quebec. "He came after the females had passed through, meaning that he had probably brought up another group of kids. He looked great. I mean, think of it . . . He flies nine thousand miles between breeding grounds and wintering grounds twice a year. It is almost beyond comprehension. Eighteen or twenty years in a row? How do you explain something like that? Maybe you can't. Maybe there is no explanation. Maybe it's just enough to know that there is such an athlete among the animals of the earth. What more can you say? . . . B95 is mind-blasting!"

Ken Ross (*left*) and
Guy Morrison (*right*)
with one of their pilots,
preparing to census
shorebirds at the
bottom of the world

GUY MORRISON
AND KEN ROSS

Dr. R. I. Guy Morrison and Ken Ross, biologists for the Canadian Wildlife Service, felt deeply attached to the shorebirds that arrived in the Canadian Arctic to breed each June. Like their American colleague Brian Harrington, they suspected that great numbers of shorebirds flew to the same little-known and unmapped places year after year. Morrison and Ross decided to go find them. Between 1982 and 1986 the two scientists flew over the entire coastline of South America in small planes, counting shorebirds from low altitudes as they went. They mapped and photographed the best sites they found.

It was dangerous work. Since neither man had a pilot's license, they had to rely on local pilots they didn't know, instructing them to fly very low. They chartered planes in unknown condition, some without radios. Sometimes pilots missed dirt landing strips or flew the little planes into violent storms, sending heads cracking against the cockpit ceiling and cameras bouncing around the cabin. "A good landing," Ken Ross observed, "is one you walk away from."

But their great circuit yielded amazing gifts. On the afternoon of January 29, 1985, while flying over Chilean Tierra del Fuego, Morrison and Ross came upon a broad bay identified on the map only as Bahía Lomas. They rounded a corner and the coast widened into a muddy intertidal zone several miles wide. The sound of the plane sent a great flock of red knots twisting up into the air before them. "It was something like seven thousand birds," Morrison recalls. As they continued along the shoreline, cloud after cloud of knots rose up before their eyes. "We counted forty-two thousand knots there," Morrison says. "We had discovered the main wintering area for *rufa* red knots in South America."

By the end of their project, the two scientists had counted almost 3 million shorebirds. They mapped the best sites and published the results in a two-volume report entitled *Atlas of Nearctic Shorebirds on the Coast of South America.* The work of the two rugged Canadian scientists led to a dream—the establishment in 1985 of the Western Hemisphere Shorebird Reserve Network, a network identifying and providing protection for key sites used by shorebirds throughout the western hemisphere.

Flying high above an enormous tidal flat, Guy Morrison took this, the first photo ever of knots at Bahía Lomas. Morrison estimated that they saw 42,000 *rufa* red knots that day. "We had discovered the main wintering area for *rufa* red knots in South America," he later said

Chapter Seven

SOUTHBOUND: CLOSING THE CIRCUIT

September–October: Mingan Archipelago, Quebec, to Tierra del Fuego, Argentina, with a stop at Maranhão, Brazil

Knots never experience real winter at any latitude. They always stay just one flight ahead of the nether parts of the calendar, alighting only when and where the larder is full, living out their lives in perpetual spring and summer. —Brian Harrington

You can practically set your calendar by B95. From October to the end of February, he is feeding on the spat-chocked restinga beaches of Rio Grande, in Tierra del Fuego, Argentina. In late May lucky observers spot him at Delaware Bay. Two weeks later, blubbery with horseshoe-crab-egg fuel, he blasts on to the Canadian Arctic, arriving just in time for the explosion of insects that fuels shorebird reproduction. And from there, for the past five years at least, he has turned up in August at Quebec's Mingan Archipelago—usually in the company of other new dads.

Soon he'll be heading back to South America, trying to reach his wintering grounds at Rio Grande, where we first met him. How will he get there? Will he attempt a marathon nonstop flight of several days and nights over the stormy Atlantic Ocean, or will he skip down the North Atlantic coast to get closer to South America before launching? If so, where will he stop?

Perhaps the most dangerous flight of all for *rufa* is a September southbound flight from Mingan to the north coast of South America. The distance is enormous, and birds must fly over the open Atlantic at a time when warm ocean waters spawn big storms and turbulent air

GEOLOCATORS

At this moment we can only make an educated guess, but a revolutionary new tool may someday show us exactly where B95 goes during the course of a year. In the spring of 2009, shorebird scientists fastened miniature, lightweight recording devices (about as heavy as a paper clip) called geolocators to the legs of forty-eight red knots captured at Delaware Bay. A geolocator contains a clock, a microprocessor, a memory chip, and a battery. At first, the devices were too heavy to fit any but the biggest of birds, but the revolution in computers has continually miniaturized the instruments until they have become light enough for even a knot to carry. Geolocators record changing light levels wherever the bird may be by providing two readings each day. The length of daylight indicates the bird's latitude. The other reading, the time when the sun reaches its highest peak in the sky, shows longitude. The two readings combined pinpoint the bird's location against the surface of the earth.

A banded or flagged bird seen in one place and then observed again somewhere else shows that a journey has taken place, but it tells nothing about the details of the trip.

A knot wearing a geolocator. If researchers can recapture it, the device will reveal every place the bird has been since the geolocator was first applied, and the routes the bird took between stops

Storms over the Atlantic during hurricane season 2010. The biggest storms include, left to right, hurricanes Karl, Igor, and Julia

In contrast, the geolocator records the journey itself: how far the bird went, the path it took, and the time of day it flew. The *voyage* is revealed. If scientists can recapture birds wearing geolocators—a big if, since knots are hard to catch even once—they can retrieve the data and use computer programs to map exactly where these birds have been.

Three of the first forty-eight red knots fitted with geolocators in May 2009 were recaptured the following May at Delaware Bay. The data give fascinating portraits of migratory flights. The first surprise was the sheer distance *rufa* can fly without stopping: in the spring, one knot flew 5,000 miles nonstop between Uruguay and the coast of North Carolina. Then, after an Arctic summer, the bird completed a flight of 3,167 miles between Canada's Hudson Bay and an island in the Caribbean. Steadily drawing down fuel, the bird stayed aloft for eight days. In all, the knot traveled a jaw-dropping 16,590 miles in 2009–10, a distance two thirds of the way around Earth's equator.

The geolocators also made it clear that *rufa* red knots don't always migrate in straight lines. One bird flew 620 miles off course to outrun a tropical storm, then, when danger passed, recalculated its position in midair and flew back to its original course.

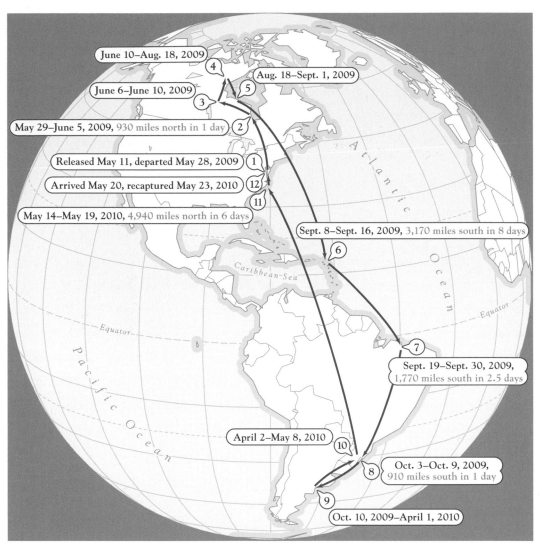

June 10–Aug. 18, 2009

④

Aug. 18–Sept. 1, 2009

⑤

June 6–June 10, 2009

③

May 29–June 5, 2009, 930 miles north in 1 day

②

Released May 11, departed May 28, 2009

①

Arrived May 20, recaptured May 23, 2010

⑫

⑪

May 14–May 19, 2010, 4,940 miles north in 6 days

Sept. 8–Sept. 16, 2009, 3,170 miles south in 8 days

⑥

Sept. 19–Sept. 30, 2009, 1,770 miles south in 2.5 days

⑦

April 2–May 8, 2010

⑩

Oct. 3–Oct. 9, 2009, 910 miles south in 1 day

⑧

⑨

Oct. 10, 2009–April 1, 2010

This map depicts the year-long journeys and stops of a red knot fitted with a geolocator on May 11, 2009, at Delaware Bay, and recaptured at Delaware Bay on May 23, 2010. The bird's astounding circuit included one northbound marathon of nearly 5,000 miles during which the bird stayed aloft for six days

Another knot took off from New Jersey, probably headed southeast over the Atlantic, but was shoved north all the way to Massachusetts by tropical storm Danny. It finally broke free at Cape Cod and started back out over the Atlantic, where it plowed into another storm, battled it for three days, and finally dropped exhausted onto an island in the Lesser Antilles. There it remained for a week, mustering fuel and strength for a three-day flight to the northern coast of Brazil, where it spent the winter.

The first three geolocator birds challenged many scientific assumptions. Researchers found themselves wondering: Have we underestimated the distance these birds can travel?

Are they taking such long flights because that's what they usually do, or are new circumstances such as climate change warming the water and causing more frequent and powerful storms? As for B95, how far has he *really* flown? When we call him Moonbird, we've been totaling up the distances he has flown in straight lines. But we're learning that migration flights rarely happen in straight lines. Could it be that the Moonbird has really flown to the moon . . . and back?

SHORT OR LONG?

Which southbound route from Mingan will B95 take? *Rufa* knots seem to divide themselves into "short distance" and "long distance" migrants on their southbound journey after breeding. About 60 percent migrate all the way to Tierra del Fuego to spend their winter months. The stamina and navigational ability required for a bird of four ounces to fly so far through such turbulent air cause biologists to rank this journey as one of the most awesome migration feats in all the animal kingdom.

A second, smaller group of *rufa* knots flies only as far as Florida, or to Caribbean beaches, and winters there. A third group seems to split the difference, wintering on the northern coast of South America but not venturing all the way to the bottom of the continent. Mingan is especially important to long-haul knots, many of which launch their nonstop transatlantic flights to South America from the shores of the Mingan Archipelago. Knots that bypass Mingan adopt a more southerly route from the Arctic, stopping to feed along the marshy shores and muddy intertidal flats of Canada's James Bay, and then on to beaches and flats along the U.S. Atlantic coast.

Whatever their southbound strategy, all knots need at least sixty days in one place to molt their flight feathers. Some remain in one place along the way, molt, and then continue south. Others wait to molt until they reach their final destination. Molting takes too much energy to accomplish while migrating. Wing feathers are brittle as they grow, because the sheath out of which each feather emerges is filled with blood. They can break under stress. Attempting an odyssey with a missing feather—a gap in the wing— would spell doom.

B95 is a classic long-haul migrant, engineered and programmed to fly the greatest of distances. His routine is consistent: for the past five years, after Arctic breeding he has flown straight to Mingan, the main terminal for transatlantic flights. Once there, he regrows his gizzard and sets about gorging on mussels and clams to put on fat for fuel. Experience has proved that he can reach Patagonia with the feathers he has. If this year is typical, he'll make the flight first, then molt at his leisure in Tierra del Fuego.

B95: THE OLDEST *RUFA* RED KNOT EVER KNOWN

When Yves Aubry spotted him on August 19, 2010, B95 became the oldest *rufa* red knot on record. B95 was first captured in 1995 and was in adult plumage then, which occurs in the third year. So when Dr. Aubry saw him, B95 was at least eighteen. The previous record holder was a *rufa* red knot banded as a juvenile in Argentina in October 1987 and recaptured in Chile in February 2003, making it sixteen.

There are at least two other records of non-*rufa* knots reaching twenty. One was raised as a pet. In February 1980, a Dutch couple discovered a red knot with a broken wing on the seashore. They took it home to their cottage in a coastal village and took care of it until it died in January 2000. Its daily routine was always the same. It got up around 6:00 a.m., took a freshwater bath, ate a breakfast of small crushed mussels, along with a serving of minced beef, which it repeated in the evening. It slept in an open box with clean sand. Every afternoon it spent an hour or two probing a loaf of fresh bread, probably to exercise its sensitive bill. Though the bird was housebound, it continued to burst into breeding plumage each year. It warned its human hosts with a loud cry whenever a raptor flew over the house.

As summer winds down and day length lessens, familiar stirrings grip B95. He joins a restless flock forming on a Mingan island shore, feeding and jabbering and pacing. They boomerang as a unit out over the water and snap back to shore again. Then they do it again, and again. Sometime in the late afternoon of a September day, a front passes through Acadian Canada. He and several other veteran migrants utter sharp, distinctive calls and raise their wings to the wind. Realization shivers through the flock that this is it: we're going. The beach seethes with the motion of wing beats. Some knots are so heavy with fat they require running starts to take off, like a full plane needing a long runway. B95 takes a place in the fold, lifts up with the others in tightening circles high over the island shore, sets his bearings by swinging with his flock mates back and forth a few times, and banks with a steady determination to the southeast.

Once again, we have no geolocator to tell us B95's exact route south, but there are enough data from banded knots to inform an educated guess. Here's how the journey might have gone: The St. Lawrence River fades behind them as B95 and his flock shape themselves into a V, passing high over the already-white fields of Nova Scotia until they finally gain the open waters of the Atlantic. Soon the gray and pleated sea also disappears from sight as the sun slips below the horizon and they move chattering through the darkness together.

Their destination is a Brazilian coastal mangrove ecosystem near the mouth of the Amazon River. Maranhão, a frequent destination for southbound *rufa* knots, is some 3,700 miles from Mingan. With 60 grams of newly laid fat, B95 has packed nearly one hundred hours' worth of fuel. Traveling at speeds of 40 miles an hour, and if he encounters no hurricanes or major storms—a very big if—he should have enough fuel to make it.

B95 and the other knots gain altitude and speed as they streak over the ocean, following the warm Gulf Stream. Pumping their wings several beats per second, they cut through high, thin air, advancing on the downstroke, lifting on the up. Burdened with fat, they stroke hard and fly at a rapid speed to maintain altitude.

By the second day they clear the Gulf Stream and enter the mid-Atlantic. There are no landmarks to guide them now—just water from horizon to horizon. B95 and the others do their best to track south, but a swiftly moving storm born in western Africa, which has been gaining strength over the Atlantic for several days, pushes them eastward. They fly through stinging rain until the air stabilizes, and then resume along a southwesterly course. They rejoin their initial path in the still, heavy air over the Sargasso Sea. Below them is an endless floating meadow of brown algae. They pump their wings furiously to keep up speed.

At nightfall, constellations of the northern sky fade behind them and new star clusters take their place in the southern sky ahead. After a third continuous day and night of exertion, B95's feathers are worn and frayed. His wing tendons are stressed almost to the tearing point, and he is panting for oxygen. But the flock pushes on, at last entering tropical latitudes, where it receives a welcome boost from warm trade winds that blow stiffly from the northeast. At last, far ahead, a straight line of puffy white clouds tops the Brazilian coast. The great Amazon River, sluggish and brown, emerges through the coastal haze. With the end in sight, the panting birds accelerate like runners stretching for the tape. It is a flock of much leaner birds—animals who just four days earlier were feeding in northern Canada—that flashes into the view of coastal fishermen. B95 tucks his wings for landing, and glides once again onto the thick brown mud of South America's crown.

B95 and the flock linger a few days to refuel, then resume their southbound odyssey. For many hours they wing over the deep green canopy of the Amazon rain forest. After hundreds of miles, the first snowy Andean peaks shimmer into view on the right and remain to escort them down the long Patagonian coast. Eventually they reach the brown, tapering bottom of South America and flash over the hard-blue Magellan Strait. Finally over Tierra del Fuego, they set their sights upon the familiar curve of the Rio Grande. And then, there it is at last, a red smudge of restinga. B95 and his mates zigzag into a glide and slap down onto the red, spat-filled pavement, where they will spend the next months until the circle begins again.

In October 2010, researchers started patrolling the beaches of Rio Grande, peering through telescopes and binoculars, counting the knots that had returned, and scanning for the Moonbird. On February 23, 2011, Luis Benegas, a skilled and persistent observer who has perhaps seen B95 more than anyone else, planted his spotting scope above a beach near Rio Grande to sort through a flock of shorebirds that had gathered there. He screwed his scope onto its tripod, peered into his lens, and found himself staring at B95. He put a camera to his scope and snapped a photo that quickly found its way around the world.

It was inspiring news, though at least one biologist noted that February 23 was a late date for B95 to still be feeding at Rio Grande. Shouldn't he be headed north by now? That was the last time he was seen at Rio Grande that "winter," and likewise he escaped notice at Delaware Bay the following May. Concern grew when he was not observed at Mingan, a place he is regularly seen in late summer.

The flocks of *rufa* knots that trickled into Rio Grande in the autumn of 2011 were small and widely scattered. There was no sign of B95 in October. People began to remind themselves that nothing lives forever. If he was alive, B95 would be nearly twenty years old by now, a veteran of countless punishing flights, flights that had to be growing more difficult for him all the time. What a life he had lived!

On the morning of November 9, a small flock of shorebirds settled in the intertidal zone before a cluster of monuments to soldiers who had lost their lives in the Falkland Islands War of 1982. Squinting hard through his scope, Luis Benegas observed a red knot bearing B95's distinctive combination of bands and flags, but the bird was too far away to capture in a clear photo. Twice again in the next weeks, Luis and a fellow observer, Tabaré Barreto, saw the same bird but could not get close enough to snap a photo that would confirm the sighting.

Just before noon on November 25, about two hundred shorebirds—knots, godwits, plovers, and sandpipers—rode a stiff breeze into the intertidal zone of a reddish Rio Grande beach near a sewage treatment plant. Luis Benegas and Tabaré Barreto stood waiting, collars turned up against a steady rain that slicked the restinga into a glistening pavement. They saw him right away, this time too close to miss. There he was, eagerly yanking spat from the restinga shelves, flying nimbly away from oncoming waves. He appeared to be in fine condition. It occurred to Luis that after seventeen years and hundreds of thousands of miles, B95 was now only three miles away from the beach where he was first banded in 1995. At 12:29 p.m., Benegas snapped the photo that confirmed B95's survival and soon gladdened hearts throughout the world.

It was inspiring news, proving that the sacred places and ancient routes that make up *rufa*'s annual circuit to the breeding grounds and back had sustained this amazing aviator for another year. To be sure, some stepping-stones were crowded, littered with trash, and depleted of food, but each place still had enough protein to send him on to the next refueling station. Though the air was violent at times, no gust or storm could match his will to live and reproduce. He shot through powerful winds and sheets of rain. No germ or virus or red tide defeated him. No falcon could track him down.

For one more year the oldest and most successful *rufa* red knot had completed his Great Circuit around the western hemisphere. And in all likelihood, soon, chubby with spat fuel, he will once again pace the restinga impatiently until the wind fills his feathers and lifts him off to begin yet another circuit. The ultimate long-distance flyer, B95 *is* the Moonbird. More than that, he is the symbol of hope for those throughout the world who love shorebirds.

Now the question is: Will his offspring have a chance to continue this amazing tenure on the wind? Much of the answer depends upon us.

Luis Benegas proved that B95 had once again completed his hemispheric circuit with this photo taken at Rio Grande, November 25, 2011

Chapter Eight

EXTINCTION IS FOREVER

When the last individual of a race of living things breathes no more, another heaven and another earth must pass before such a one can be again.
　　　　　　　　　　　　—William Beebe, from *The Bird: Its Form and Function*

To become extinct is the greatest tragedy in all nature. Extinction means that all the members of an entire genetic family are dead and gone, forever. Some might argue that this doesn't seem so tragic. After all, according to scientists, 99 percent of all species that have ever lived are now extinct. And during the last half-billion years there have already been five big waves of mass extinction, when at least two-thirds of all species alive at the time disappeared quickly. These episodes were caused by everything from volcanic eruptions to drought.

The fifth and most recent mass extinction took place a mere 65 million years ago, when an asteroid collided with Earth, sending fiery dust into the atmosphere and suddenly cooling the planet, eliminating the dinosaurs and most other animal species alive at the time (although not the horseshoe crab, as we have seen). In other words, mass extinction is nothing new; we've been through this before.

But the sixth wave, the one that's happening now, is different. For the first time a single species, *Homo sapiens*—humankind—is wiping out thousands of life-forms by consuming and altering the earth's resources. Humans now consume more than half of the world's freshwater and nearly half of everything that's grown on the land. Though we've been clearing land and planting food crops for only a few thousand years, our impact upon the earth is so deep, and accelerating so rapidly, that thousands of species are vanishing every year. According to scientists at the University of California, Berkeley, if current rates of extinction continue, Earth could lose *three quarters* of its species within the next three hundred years. Some are famous and beloved—such as the lions of Kenya and the tigers of India—but most are small and obscure.

Each species belongs to a complicated web of energy and activity called an ecosystem. Together, these webs connect everything from microorganisms to mighty trees. We are only now beginning to understand how these systems work, and what species within ecosystems mean to one another. What could happen if a particular species is removed from an ecosystem? Could the whole ecosystem unravel? It's probably best not to find out. As the conservationist Aldo Leopold put it, "The first rule of an intelligent tinkerer is to keep all of the pieces."

B95 is a bird of the sixth wave. Though he is able to transform his body to meet his needs, rapidly shifting human activities have challenged his ability to keep up with broader changes in his world. B95's story gives us a chance to learn more about the native plants and animals around us, and to ask ourselves, "What can we do to protect them before it's too late?"

What will it take to save *rufa* from extinction?

SAVING THE *RUFA* RED KNOT

What will it take to save *rufa* from extinction? How will B95's descendants remain among us? In fact, will there be any shorebirds *at all* along the earth's coastlines in the years ahead? These are serious questions: now nearly half the world's shorebird species are declining, and shorebirds have become the most endangered migratory birds of all. The main reason? Many of the best stopover sites for migratory shorebirds—their magnet-like stepping-stones—are being littered with trash, crowded with much bigger creatures and machines, raced over, dug up, polluted, poisoned, and otherwise degraded so that the birds' needs cannot be met.

To save B95's descendants, the governments, business leaders, and ordinary citizens—young and old—of a dozen or so nations will have to unite to protect places scattered throughout two continents. A single break in the circuit could cause the whole system to collapse. Leaders and volunteers will have to learn from shorebirds, recognizing no boundaries at all. Future B95s must depend on abundant food and a safe place to roost after a long journey—in exactly the right places.

There is reason for hope. After more than thirty years of exploration, many of the *rufa* stepping-stone sites have at long last been discovered and mapped. The discoverers—scientists such as Brian Harrington, Larry Niles, Amanda Dey, Guy Morrison, Allan Baker, Patricia González, and Yves Aubry—have built networks of volunteers to count and band the birds and keep track of their well-being. Twenty thousand *rufa* red knots have been banded since 1997 alone (with B-95 the only known survivor of a banding effort even before that). Many have been resighted at least once. The *rufa* red knot may be the best-studied shorebird of all.

Work to protect *rufa* has already started, although at this writing the population

WHSRN SITES

Some of *rufa*'s most important stopover sites have received international recognition. When a site is named in the Western Hemisphere Shorebird Reserve Network (WHSRN), it means that scientists from several nations agree that this site is among the most important to shorebirds. Sometimes, WHSRN attention has turned into legal protection. For example, Lagoa do Peixe, the shallow Brazilian lagoon where knots stop to tank up on tiny snails during their northbound migration, became a Brazilian national park after having first been named a WHSRN site. The first WHSRN site was Delaware Bay, named in 1985.

For the red knot and other shorebirds to survive, their breeding and stopover habitats will have to be preserved throughout the world, such as in the nature reserve on the Atlantic coast of Tierra del Fuego marked by this sign

has dropped to a dangerously low level. There are now restrictions on the number of horseshoe crabs that can be taken from Delaware Bay—with special measures to protect female crabs. In Argentina, two Patagonian provinces—Santa Cruz and Rio Negro—have passed laws making it illegal for anyone to modify a wetland important to shorebirds. A plan to add further protection for shorebirds at San Antonio Bay is being written. The Chilean national oil company, ENAP, has stopped oil and gas production at Bahía Lomas—the prime wintering site for *rufa* knots. The company has also donated free helicopter time to help biologists conduct surveys of shorebirds. *Rufa* has been declared endangered in Argentina, soon will be in Canada, and is in line in the United States—though the process is painfully slow.

YOUTH GET INVOLVED

No one understands thinking beyond national boundaries better than young people today. Empowered by cell phones, the Internet, and social networking, they are helping red knots and other shorebirds in various ways. Here are a few things happening around the world.

Las Grutas, Argentina. Twelve-year-old Luciana Cec-cacci fell in love with red knots after her parents took her to the beach to see them at Las Grutas one winter day. She has since learned how to band shore-birds. Luciana spends much of her free time volunteer-ing at Vuelo Latitud 40, a museum and education center in Las Grutas. Luciana won a literary prize for

Luciana Ceccacci, Argentine author of "A Bird?"

her essay "A Bird?" about a child who woke up one morning as a red knot. In her story, Luciana takes the reader on a migratory flight, encountering the factors that are driving *rufa* toward extinction. Her story has now been published as a children's picture book in Argentina and made into a prize-winning play.

Delaware Bay, USA. Friends of the Red Knot. Mike Hudson, a birder from Baltimore, learned about the red knot's distress on an Audubon Society bird walk in 2007. After online research, Mike and three friends made a school presentation on the red knot, generating enough interest to form a club dedicated to saving it.

Mike Hudson, founder of Friends of the Red Knot, holds a red knot in breeding plumage during a banding operation

Friends of the Red Knot launched a letter-writing campaign to the U.S. Fish and Wildlife Service, urging that *rufa* be listed as an endangered species. With skillful use of the Internet, their appeal for listing has spread widely and rapidly. Their Web site is www.friendsoftheredknot.org. Friends of the Red Knot is, at this writing, shifting its focus to education, trying to help students recognize shorebirds, care about them, and help to protect their habitats.

Patagonia, Argentina. RARE Pride Campaigns. Working at three stepping-stone sites for *rufa*, young people are helping RARE Conservation to shape community attitudes toward shorebirds. At San Antonio, the task is to protect intertidal beach habitat from disturbances caused by 4×4 vehicles on beaches where knots feed. Young workers inform beach visitors (residents and tourists) of the beach's importance to birds and the threats posed by this disturbance. The goal is to reduce daily disturbances by 60 percent and to ensure that 25 percent of the entire red knot population continues to use the beach as a stopover site. Young workers are also at the heart of campaigns at the Rio Gallegos Estuary and at the Costa Atlantica de Tierra del Fuego, where the effort is to control trash and other solid waste on the beach. For more about RARE Pride Campaigns, see page 121.

EXTINCTION: A NEW IDEA

In 1705 an enormous tooth weighing five pounds, with distinctive grinding knobs on the surface, was discovered along the Hudson River in New York. It was puzzling: no one knew of such a tooth in the jaw of any living animal. Years later, similar teeth showed up in the Hudson and Ohio River valleys, baffling the likes of George Washington, Ben Franklin, and Thomas Jefferson. Even more disturbing, such a discovery shook the idea that God had already created all forms of life that could possibly be created, and arranged them in perfect order—lowest to highest—from jellyfish to worms to insects up to humans. In January 1796, the French anatomist Georges Cuvier rocked the scientific world by presenting a lecture describing his comparisons of elephant teeth of several species. He declared that the tooth had come from a new species, which he called the mastodon. Soon there was more: by carefully analyzing newly discovered fossils, Cuvier also introduced the notion of mass extinctions, during which "living organisms without number" had disappeared forever. Cuvier's work, not pleasant to accept, led, as one scientist wrote, to "the development of fundamentally new ways of thinking."

Quebec, Canada. Eleventh-grade students in the Canadian province of Quebec are working with Parks Canada to inform Canadians about the red knot's ecology and plight. An animated feature tracing the red knot's migration journey is in production. Each participating student will create a tool to educate local citizens about the knot. The tool can be a poster, a flyer, a PowerPoint presentation, a cartoon, a radio or television show—whatever works.

Opportunities exist for you to learn about shorebirds and to help them. You'll find Web links and other resources in the Appendix.

WHY SHOULD YOU CARE?

What good is a "peep"—what shorebirds are often called—anyway? You can't walk or feed them. B95 certainly won't curl up on your lap. Shorebirds don't even visit feeders. Why should you devote time and energy to protecting them? And why expect people to save birds when it may spell sacrifice, inconvenience, or even hardship? Why should you stay away from your favorite beach for a while, or stop racing your four-wheeler over a really good stretch of sand to save something most people can't even recognize?

Here are some thoughts:

Plants and animals keep us alive and improve our lives. Most of our medicines and foods come from wild plants and animals. As we've already seen, the horseshoe crab—whose eggs also give *rufa* a chance to reproduce—has helped teach us how human vision works and continues to keep our medicines safe from contamination. And, of course, the history of human aviation is inspired by and based on observations of how birds fly.

Each species with which we share the earth is a remarkable success story. Our job is to understand those forms of life, and keep them from slipping away

Each life form is fascinating and mysterious in its own right. A red knot changes its body to become a flight machine when it's time to fly, changes it again when it must eat soft food, and changes it again when it's time to reproduce. Can you grow a bigger brain before a big test? Stronger leg muscles right before a game or a race? Beyond that, a red knot completely swaps out its flight feathers each year, and changes color twice. Amazing!

Each species with which we share the earth is a success story. Each of our cohabitants has evolved an ingenious set of life strategies, and made them work. To live on an earth without fascinating, often beautiful creatures would be to live on a lesser earth. The trick is not to let them slip away, but to understand and help them on *their* terms. It's not easy to figure wild plants and animals out. One has to read, study, and observe them and then use one's imagination. Why would a red knot fly nine thousand miles to breed? Wouldn't it be much safer just to stay put?

An animal's size, shape, appendages, colors, loudness, odor, texture, activity, and speed all represent strategies for survival worked out over many years. If we observe thoughtfully, each survivor will reveal clues for how to help them and also, perhaps, ourselves.

Most of the world is useless to B95. He'll drown if he lands on the sea. The Brazilian rain forest offers him nothing. The farmland behind the shore is meaningless. The few scattered addresses that draw him as if he is magnetized to them are all he has. What those places have in common is the presence of food at a certain moment and enough light in the sky for him to see his prey as long as possible. For nearly twenty years now, B95 has followed a ripple of food and a beam of light across the globe, just as his ancestors did long before.

Will B95 live to see the time when there are as many *rufa* alive as there were when he was born? It seems unlikely. He's nearly twenty years old as I write these words.

Extinction is the greatest tragedy in nature. Will B95's descendants be able to continue?

That's a long time for a knot to live. But it's possible. One knot of another subspecies lived to be at least twenty-five. If we work hard, and if he continues the steady habits that have made him the most successful of all known living shorebirds, maybe B95 will still be with us when his sacred places are secure, inspiring us in his own way by simply enduring as the eldest of his tribe, the ultimate citizen of the wind.

Mike Hudson, founder of Friends of the Red Knot, tightens his focus on a shorebird at Delaware Bay

MIKE HUDSON
Founder, Friends of the Red Knot

When I was five or six my grandpa would take me to the kitchen to look through the window. There were tons of birds on the feeders in the backyard. "Have you ever really looked at the birds, Mike?" he'd say. Well, I hadn't. Then he taught me how to draw them. I really grew to love birds that way.

When I was ten I went on a bird walk in Baltimore, and the leader started talking about a project he was working on to save the red knot. He said it was a migratory shorebird that used Delaware Bay. The next week there was an article in the paper about it. Three friends and I decided we'd do something at school to help it. This was in 2007, when the red knot was really crashing and some thought it would be extinct by 2010. To me, it was a natural next step to help them. My question was, "If we can stop this, why don't we?"

I arranged for an ornithologist to come to school and speak about the knots. There was a lot of interest. About fifteen to twenty kids agreed to help, even kids in first grade. My dad gave us advice about how to draft letters and petitions, how to contact officials.

Our goal was to get the red knot listed as an endangered species. We researched the law and knew it met the criteria. We wrote postcards every day to the secretary of the interior. We formed a group, Friends of the Red Knot. We set up a display at the DuPont Nature Center on Delaware Bay. We went to Gandy's Beach at Delaware Bay and observed the birds. Some of us joined in a banding team and we actually got to *hold* them. It was an *unbelievable* experience!

We made presentations and testified at hearings to try to give the red knot protection in the states surrounding Delaware Bay. We got results. Six of us took turns reading testimony at a hearing sponsored by the Delaware Department of Natural Resources. We asked for a ban on horseshoe crab harvesting, or, at the least, tight restrictions. They did tighten restrictions. Friends of the Red Knot was invited to speak to the Baltimore City Council. I represented us. Then the council passed a resolution commending Friends of the Red Knot and supporting the listing of the red knot as an endangered species.

Fishermen also testified, and I heard their point of view. When I volunteered at the Nature Center, just about every day this one fisherman would come in, and we would talk. He made me understand his point of view. Sometimes it was very hard to talk with someone whose tradition and livelihood might be lost if crab restrictions were imposed. I still thought something had to be done, but maybe we had to think more broadly to accomplish our goals.

Now I'm fifteen and a freshman in high school. And now I lead bird walks, rather than always being led. Friends of the Red Knot is about to enter a new phase, where we emphasize networking and public education. I get kids interested now. I started a bird club at my school with a teacher. We take trips to the shore. We want kids to notice the little feathered creatures on the beach. If they notice them, you can tell the kids things about them that will get them interested. And if they're interested, they will come to care. And if they come to care, they will act on a bird's behalf. That's how Friends of the Red Knot works. I didn't start with theories or bird textbooks. I brought kids outside.

APPENDIX: WHAT YOU CAN DO

KNOW YOUR BIRDS

Learn to identify birds, starting with the common birds around your neighborhood. If you can confidently tell a robin from a cardinal or a blue jay, you've taken an important first step. Make a list of the bird species you can recognize. Pick up a bird field guide—a book or app that has photos or drawings of birds and explains how to identify them. Go outside and give it a try. You'll do better with binoculars, but these are not absolutely

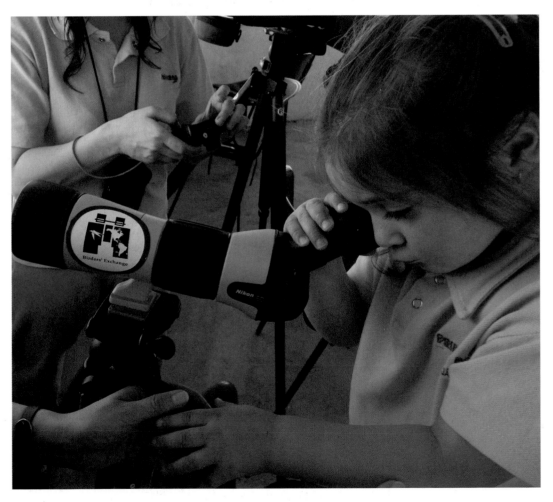

Learn your birds; it's never too early to start!

necessary if you're a good observer and notice details. You can even learn to identify birds by the sounds they make. There are good apps of birdsongs that can be downloaded into any computer, iPod, or smartphone.

The quickest way to learn is to study with people who know more than you. Go on bird walks with others. Most cities have Audubon Societies, organizations dedicated to understanding and conserving birds. I go out with an Audubon group on Thursday mornings to sharpen my own observation skills. Here is a link to the National Audubon Society: www.audubon.org. Their Web site page "Audubon Near You" will tell you whether there is an Audubon group in your area. Even if there is no organized group where you live, there are people around you who know about birds. Find them. Start a bird club of your own.

If you live near the ocean, head for the beach and tackle shorebird identification. Peeps can be very tricky. Look at their size and coloring, the coloring of their feet, and the length and shape of the bill. See if you can tell a plover from a sandpiper. Practiced birders detect whether a bird is an adult or juvenile by examining its feathering.

SOME PROJECTS FOR YOUNG BIRDERS

The Shorebird Sister Schools Program. Some years ago an Alaskan schoolteacher got the idea to build an information-sharing e-mail network linking schools located all along the Pacific migratory flyway. The network would connect students from Alaska to Latin America. Students from each migratory stopover site could report their observations by sending e-mail messages to all other schools participating in the program. And it worked! Starting in 1994, seventeen schools from Alaska to California were connected to the shorebird information network. Now the network is managed by the U.S. Fish and Wildlife Service and has grown to include schools from all across the USA, several Latin American countries, Japan, and Russia. There's a shorebird conservation curriculum available free of charge to any school, in English, Spanish, Russian, and Japanese. There is also a site on migration research. You can find bird-loving pen pals from many places throughout a particular shorebird's migratory route, and even meet them at one of the many shorebird festivals within the flyway. Here's a link: www.fws.gov/sssp.

Wandering Wildlife. Another intriguing Web site is called Wandering Wildlife. This project of the Alaska Science Center uses satellite technology to track migrating animals. An Arctic wolf named Brutus has been outfitted with a satellite collar, in order to see where his pack travels during the Arctic winter. Scientists also track shorebirds by satellite as they migrate across oceans and continents. Visit the Web site alaska.usgs.gov/science/biology/wandering_wildlife/. When you click on one of the indicated species,

VUELO LATITUD 40

In Las Grutas, a seashore town in Patagonia, Argentina, you will find a building devoted entirely to learning about shorebirds. Vuelo Latitud 40 is a fun, innovative place to learn. Once inside, you follow red knot footprints through the corridors. Above your head streams a dense flock of papier-mâché knots, helping you navigate through the exhibits. Innovative ideas make it easy to learn. To make the point that a red knot can eat more than its own weight, there is a diorama of a child standing next to a mountain of hamburgers. In the Red Knot Club, you get banded and flagged, just like a knot. There are spotting scopes aimed at the seashore outside. One exhibit shows how birds use different-shaped bills to feed. By pressing a button alongside a particular month of the year, you can make a globe light up to show where *rufa* is likely to be at that time. And, with luck, you will meet Fabian, the red knot mascot named after the hero of Antoine de Saint-Exupéry's book *Night Flight.*

Volunteers, often young people,
are at the heart of many banding expeditions

it will load a series of migration routes. Once you get the message "Why is this study important?" you can click on an individual bird and watch where it traveled from day to day.

RARE *Pride Campaigns*. The organization called RARE trains local conservation leaders throughout the world to change the way their communities relate to nature. They work through Pride Campaigns—so named because they aim to inspire people to take pride in the species and habitats that make their community unique, while also introducing practical alternatives to environmentally destructive practices. Many of the Pride Campaigns involve young people. To find out more, contact RARE at www.rare conservation.org/empowering-local-communities-solve-global-conservation-challenges.

Parks Canada has created a wonderful resource to help high school students learn about red knots. Entitled "What Happened to the *Rufa* Red Knot Population?" it is available in English and French. Students follow the *rufa* throughout its migratory

Students band shorebirds and record data at Delaware Bay

circuit, discovering the disturbances affecting its population. They learn to use the capture-mark-recapture method of identifying knots and how to estimate the size of the 2008 population. Each student creates a public education tool to heighten public awareness of the shorebird and its plight. Some of the material is animated; B95 is featured. The Web site is www.parkscanada.gc.ca/education-redknot.

Friends of the Red Knot. You can work with groups that organize actions such as letter-writing campaigns to public officials, petitions, or media events. One of the best is Friends of the Red Knot, which is described on page 116 in the profile of its founder, Mike Hudson. You can reach Friends of the Red Knot at friendsoftheredknot@verizon.net.

Scientific Studies of Birds. The opportunity to work with birds in the wild, to witness their activities up close, or even to hold them in your hand can change your life. Learning to band birds is a great way to advance your understanding of birdlife and to contribute to scientific knowledge. One place to develop a serious scientific interest in birds, especially if you live in the northeastern United States, is through the banding program of the Manomet Center for Conservation Sciences. The program has been going for more than forty years. At Manomet, schoolchildren, university students, and adults can learn banding techniques, and can also gain a better understanding of local ecosystems and how to protect them. To date, about 25,000 young people have come to Manomet during the spring or fall migration to see birds up close and to learn about their habits and needs. You may reach Manomet at www.manomet.org/about-manomet/bird-observatory.

In the end, one of the most important things you can do is to develop respect for shorebirds. Study them at a distance that is safe for them. Don't spook them. Remember that every time they are flushed from a feeding position or roosting spot on a beach and forced to move elsewhere, they burn energy that they will need to replace.

Those who already have birding skills can contribute to the International Shorebird Survey. Since 1974, Manomet has been training volunteers to collect information on shorebirds, the wetlands they use, and their migratory paths. Contact the ISS at www.manomet.org /our-initiatives/shorebird-recovery-project /ISS-prism.

B95 at Rio Grande

SOURCE NOTES

The idea to write a book about B95 came from my friend Dr. Charles Duncan, a bird scientist and conservationist who works for the Manomet Center for Conservation Sciences. Charles lives near me in Maine. Fluent in Spanish, he traveled to Cuba with me when I was researching and writing *The Race to Save the Lord God Bird*, about the ivory-billed woodpecker. Charles knew I was looking for another bird species or subspecies to write about, a bird type that is in danger of becoming extinct, but one for which there is still hope. He made several suggestions, but nothing seemed quite right to me.

"What about red knots?" he said one day in 2009. "They're fabulous birds. They take unbelievably long migration flights to end-of-the-world places. They're beautiful, especially in breeding plumage. They are disappearing for reasons people need to know about. But it's not hopeless—there are still thousands left. A good book could help them."

I still wasn't sure. Stories need characters. How could I put a reader in the air with hundreds of birds that all look alike? And then came the breakthrough call. "Look," Charles said. "I was just talking to Patricia González, a biologist in Argentina. She told me about this one red knot. They first trapped and banded it in 1995. They keep seeing it. While so many others are dying, this bird keeps surviving unbelievably hard flights. There's a band around its leg that says B95. It's flown so far people are starting to call it Moonbird."

Bingo.

I decided to follow B95 around his hemispheric circuit for a year, starting in Argentina. I arrived in Rio Grande, Tierra del Fuego, Argentina, in December 2009. Next I moved on to Las Grutas on San Antonio Bay to conduct interviews. In May 2010 I traveled to Reeds Beach, Delaware Bay, to take part in shorebird catch attempts and conduct interviews. And I visited the Manomet Center for Conservation Sciences in Massachusetts to do research and interviewing.

I read widely, but most of what I learned came from my own observations and from interviews with experts. I had the enormous advantage of unrestricted access to the brilliant scientists who know the most about those birds. Some experts—Larry Niles and Yves Aubry come especially to mind—not only granted me detailed interviews but also answered dozens and dozens of follow-up questions in long e-mail messages, some tapped out while they were working in the field. Individuals I interviewed at length are listed below. An asterisk indicates more than one such interview.

*Yves Aubry, ornithologist with the Canadian Wildlife Service; *Allan Baker, vice president for the Department of Natural History for the Royal Ontario Museum; Ron Berzofsky, general manager, LAL Division, Wako Chemicals USA; Luciana Ceccacci, author of "A Bird?"; *Amanda Dey, principal zoologist for the New Jersey Endangered and Nongame Species Program; *Charles

Duncan, director of the Shorebird Recovery Project, Manoment Center for Conservation Sciences; Frank "Thumper" Eicherly, Delaware Bay waterman; *Patricia González, head of the wetlands program, Fundación Inalafquen; *Brian Harrington, biologist, Manomet Center for Conservation Sciences; Mike Hudson, founder, Friends of the Red Knot; Fred Layton, Jr., Delaware Bay waterman; *Clive Minton, Victoria Wader Study Group; *R. I. Guy Morrison, senior research scientist, National Wildlife Research Centre, Environment Canada; *Larry Niles, former chief of the New Jersey Endangered and Nongame Species Program and director of Conserve Wildlife; Theunis Piersma, head of the Animal Ecology Group, University of Groningen, the Netherlands; Silvana Sawicki, director of Vuelo, Latitud 40, Las Grutas, Argentina; Smokey Swickla, proprietor, Smokey's, Reeds Beach, New Jersey; Jan Van de Kam, wildlife photographer.

Here are the most important sources by chapter. Unless otherwise noted, references are to sources cited in the Bibliography.

CHAPTER ONE • SUPERBIRD

My interviews and work with biologists and volunteers first in Rio Grande and then in Las Grutas, Argentina, informed most of this chapter.

14 *60 percent of the entire* rufa *population.* Each year, Guy Morrison of the Canadian Wildlife Service counts "wintering" birds at Tierra del Fuego from small airplanes flying at low altitudes. His figures are combined with other fall counts at Mingan and from the U.S. Atlantic coast in fall, and from other places in *rufa*'s range, to arrive at population estimates.

15 *Why Do Red Knots Go So Far?* Interview with Dr. Clive Minton, who has been studying migratory shorebirds for decades.

18–20 *1995: The Black Band.* The story of Allan Baker's determination to learn about knots in the field rather than by collecting specimens comes from an interview with Dr. Baker. The February 20, 1995, catch at Rio Grande has become legendary among shorebird biologists. It brought together for the first time many of the figures from around the world who would lead the fight to save *rufa* when its crisis became clear. Included were Allan Baker, Theunis Piersma, Patricia González, Luis Benegas, and Clive Minton. And of course, B95. The difficulty of finding blasting powder, the huge catch, the deteriorating weather, the participation of the navy, the teenagers to the rescue—all are the stuff of lore. My narrative is pieced together from interviews with all of the above except, alas, for the feathered star of the show.

20 *Molt.* There is a fine, nicely illustrated discussion of molt in Sibley, pp. 274–77. Additionally, Allan Baker schooled me in juvenile knot feathering when I sat next to him during a banding operation on December 8, 2009. Larry Niles showed me how to read the feather wear of the bird illustrated on page 20.

21 *2001: An Identity.* Interviews with Patricia González and Allan Baker.

22 *Bands and Flags.* See the "techniques" page of www.bandedbirds.org.

21–25 *2007: The Moonbird.* From interviews with Patricia González, Allan Baker, Luis Benegas, and the biologist Mauricio Failla.

26–27 *Profile: Clive Minton.* From personal interviews.

CHAPTER TWO • THE FLIGHT MACHINE

29 *The secret is an astounding feat of bodybuilding.* Much of what I wrote about the changes a knot can make rests upon the research of Dr. Theunis Piersma, an evolutionary biologist from the Royal Netherlands Institute for Sea Research, and by the Canadian biologist Guy Morrison. There is a discussion of these changes in Morrison et al., "COSEWIC Assessment," pp. 21–22. My understanding derives mainly from interviews with both biologists.

30 *Snapping the Whip.* Brian Harrington's beautiful description of this phenomenal flocking display is found in Harrington, p. 38.

32–33 *Liftoff.* This hypothetical flight is from my imagination, based on readings and interviews with experts. We do not know B95's exact hemispheric circuit. He is a well-established regular visitor at three places: Mingan, Delaware Bay, and Rio Grande. The distances separating these points are probably too great for there not to be other stops. After discussions with biologists, I filled in the circuit with refuelings at San Antonio and Lagoa do Peixe on the northbound flight, and Maranhão on the southbound. These are educated guesses based primarily on distances from the previous stopover, habits of other knots, and the known availability of food.

33–35 *A Flying Compass.* There are fine discussions of how birds navigate and orient their position in the sky in Sibley, pp. 63–65, and Weidensaul, Chapter 3.

35 *First Stop.* My own visits to the beaches at San Antonio and Las Grutas were supplemented by interviews with Patricia González and Silvana Sawicki.

36–39 *Second Stop.* See Harrington, pp. 56–61.

40–41 *Profile: Patricia González.* From personal interviews.

CHAPTER THREE • SHOWDOWN AT DELAWARE BAY

43–47 *Night of a Full Moon . . .* There are many descriptions of the synchrony between *rufa* and *Limulus* at Delaware Bay. One of the best is the film *Crash: A Tale of Two Species.* Also see Weidensaul, pp. 304–6, and Harrington, pp. 70–77.

47–48 *1979: A Springtime Dilemma.* The story of Brian Harrington and Linda Leddy at Reeds Beach in 1979 comes from an interview with Brian Harrington in 2010. The story also appears in Sargent, pp. 73–74.

48–52 *The Ancient Giver.* William Sargent's *Crab Wars*, a fine, readable study of the horseshoe crab, its history, its exploitation, and the contributions it has made to human health, was a prime resource.

51 *Bleeding Horseshoe Crabs at a Lysate Facility.* The most informative of many interviews on this topic was with Dr. Ron Berzofsky, general manager of the LAL Division of Wako Chemicals USA, Inc.

51 *As high as 30 percent.* See "Mortality in Female Horseshoe Crabs (*Limulus polyphemus*) from Biomedical Bleeding and Handling: Implications for Fisheries Management" by A. S. Leschen and S. J. Correia, Massachusetts Division of Marine Fisheries, New Bedford, Mass.

52–54 *Cape May, New Jersey, Early Morning.* Much has been written about the impact of bait fishing on horseshoe crab populations at Delaware Bay. I tried to avoid the war of numbers—how many crabs have been taken, how many are left, what is a sustainable number of horseshoe crabs for Delaware Bay if shorebird conservation is the goal. My aim was to describe the practice of using horseshoe crabs as bait in pots lowered underwater to capture eels and whelk. I also sought to provide a sense of the marketplace, and of the fever for horseshoe crabs before some restrictions were applied. To understand the waterman's perspective I was helped by conversations with Smokey Swickla, who owns a waterman's outfitter shop and marina on the Jersey side of the bay, and by the veteran Delaware Bay fishermen Fred Layton, Jr., and Frank "Thumper" Eicherly.

Larry Niles, Clive Minton, and Allan Baker also spoke with me about this topic during inter-views.

55–57 *Profile: Brian Harrington.* From personal interviews.

CHAPTER FOUR • TWINKLING AND TRAPPING

This chapter is built upon my visit to the New Jersey side of Delaware Bay, May 21–23, 2010. I was lucky to be there on a day—May 22—when a catch was attempted, and accomplished. Catches often fizzle for various reasons. Many days it is impossible to get enough birds on one beach in front of a net. Or sometimes the weather is too foul. But this was an amazingly skillful team, and we had a gorgeous day. Many of the techniques I describe were patiently developed over the years by Dr. Clive Minton and Humphrey Sitters. Their experience and knowledge informed every bit of this complicated opera-tion. Larry Niles orchestrated a beautiful plan and Dr. Amanda Dey patiently went over every step of the operation with volunteers in advance. We were well prepared when the cannon went off.

68 *In 1997, the first year* . . . Interview with Larry Niles.

68 *Frank "Thumper" Eicherly: A Delaware Bay Waterman.* From personal interview.

70 *B95 at Delaware Bay.* The Web site www.bandedbirds.org is for scientists and informed bird-ers to report their sightings of banded birds. Since 1995 observers have been marking captured birds with color-coded bands—many with individual letter-and-number combinations. This has resulted in a large database of sightings along the Atlantic coast. Through these data we are gaining a better understanding of shorebird migration routes, and nesting and wintering areas. The site contains instructions on how to report a banded bird. Through the "Public Search" link, you can choose the correct species and flag color, then enter the marker code to see where your bird was banded and where else it has been sighted.

CHAPTER FIVE • THE ARCTIC BREEDING GROUNDS

Much of this chapter is informed by a wonderful description of *rufa* red knots in the Arctic in Harrington, pp. 84–94. Information about more recent research activity came from Larry Niles and Dr. Amanda Dey, who have been studying red knots in the Canadian Arctic for most of the past decade, especially on Southampton Island. The film *Crash: A Tale of Two Species* will show you what this amazing place looks like.

75 *Getting Ready to Reproduce.* Much of this sidebar was informed by a long telephone interview with Theunis Piersma, an evolutionary biologist from the Netherlands who studies the amazing physiological transformations knots make during particular stages of their lives.

80–81 *Profile: Amanda Dey.* From personal interview.

CHAPTER SIX • MINGAN: THE BELLWETHER SITE

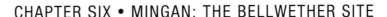

83 *On the chilly morning . . .* Interviews with Yves Aubry and Cédrik Juillet.

86 *The Mystery of the Missing Knots.* The mystery is cited in Harrington, p. 182. Information about the development of awareness of Mingan's importance came mainly from interviews with Yves Aubry.

86–87 *A Fledgling's First Journey.* I put together this account of a hypothetical flight between an island in the Canadian Arctic and Mingan using information from a wide variety of sources. That knots separate themselves into waves of females, males, and finally juveniles was established through interviews with several scientists, including Allan Baker, Amanda Dey, and Yves

Aubry—though some biologists believe that a few adult knots remain behind to help guide juvenile birds. That B95 would have made this journey as a first-year bird is supported by the fact that he appeared at Mingan each year between 2006 and 2010. Yves Aubry helped me create a visual image of what the birds can see below them as they travel. He sent me maps and photos, and talked me through the journey by telephone.

89 *Herbst Corpuscles . . .* Herbst corpuscles are described in Harrington's notes, p. 177.

90–91 *Missing.* Interview with Yves Aubry.

92–93 *Profile: Guy Morrison and Ken Ross.* From interview with R. I. Guy Morrison.

CHAPTER SEVEN • SOUTHBOUND: CLOSING THE CIRCUIT

97–100 *Geolocators.* See Larry Niles's scientific paper, as well as Sandy Bauers's fine article in the *Philadelphia Inquirer* about the breakthrough advantages of geolocators in tracking long-distance migratory shorebirds. Interviews with Larry Niles supplemented this information, as did Niles's blog "A Rube with a View."

100–105 *Short or Long?* See Niles's scientific paper, referenced above.

101 *The Oldest Rufa Red Knot Ever Known.* See Morrison et al., "Cosewic Assessment," pp. 20–21.

102 *Their destination is a Brazilian . . .* This hypothetical flight from Mingan to Maranhão, and then on to Rio Grande, is based on our knowledge that B95 routinely departs south from Mingan. Most Mingan birds fly out over the Atlantic rather than tracing the coast for southern destinations. It is well documented that Maranhão is an important southbound knot destination, so I put B95 there. We also know he spends the months that we know as winter in Rio Grande, so I sent him there on one long, nonstop flight from Maranhão. Fred Bodsworth's *Last of the Curlews*, published in 1954, gave ideas about the winds shorebirds are likely to encounter over the Atlantic during southbound migratory flights.

104 *On the morning of November 9 . . .* Luis Benegas described his February 23, 2011, and November 25, 2011, sightings of B95 in e-mails to interested parties, and later in e-mail interviews with me.

CHAPTER EIGHT • EXTINCTION IS FOREVER

I have worked as a conservationist for the Nature Conservancy since 1977. At the Conservancy our job is to preserve the forms of life on Earth by protecting the lands and waters they need to survive. Right now my work focuses on the central coast of British Columbia, in a magical place called the Great Bear Rainforest. I get to see grizzly bears, wolves, eagles, humpbacked whales, and many other animals as part of my job. We work with local partners, especially the Heiltsuk and Git Ga'at First Nations, to increase the opportunities young people have to learn about nature through camps, school programs, and summer internships.

In my conservation work, and in much of my writing, I have been concerned with preventing the terrible, preventable tragedy of extinction. In this chapter I offer my own thoughts, and those of others, about how to address the great global crisis of species loss.

109–110 *There is reason for hope.* Much of the information on conservation successes comes from an interview with Charles Duncan of the Manomet Center for Conservation Sciences.

112 *Extinction: A New Idea.* Much of this sidebar is informed by the article "Lost and Gone Forever," by Richard Conniff, which appeared in *The New York Times* of February 3, 2011.

116–117 *Profile: Mike Hudson.* From personal interview.

BIBLIOGRAPHY

I consulted many Web sites, articles, films, and books as I researched this book. The following were among the most helpful.

BOOKS

Bodsworth, Fred. *Last of the Curlews.* New York: Dodd, Mead & Company, 1954. Reissued April 2011. An elegant, classic work of fiction about the last surviving individual of a shorebird species—the Eskimo curlew—once abundant but now probably extinct.

Harrington, Brian, with Charles Flowers. *The Flight of the Red Knot.* New York: W. W. Norton and Company, 1996. Beautifully written and filled with stirring photographs. Harrington fills the pages with insight from decades of experience as a shorebird biologist.

Heinrich, Bernd. *Why We Run: A Natural History.* New York: HarperCollins, 2001. This discussion of why humans are motivated to run long distances contains a fascinating chapter on migrating birds.

Matthiessen, Peter. *Wildlife in America.* New York: Viking Press, 1964. A detailed survey of endangered species in the United States up to the 1960s. There is an insightful section on shorebirds.

Morrison, R.I.G., and R. K. Ross. *Atlas of Nearctic Shorebirds on the Coast of South America, Volumes 1 and 2.* Ottawa: Canadian Wildlife Service, 1989. Here are the results, in map and text form, of Morrison and Ross's historic 1982–86 flights along the South American coast. Much of what is known about important South American shorebird concentration points derives from these flights.

Saint-Exupéry, Antoine de. *Night Flight.* New York: Harcourt, 1932. Best known for his children's classic *The Little Prince*, the author was also a pioneering aviator. During the 1930s he delivered the mail by plane to small cities throughout Patagonia, frequently crossing the Andes in small planes that had very few instruments. *Night Flight* gives us a gallant hero, Fabian, and beautiful passages about the magic and terror of flight.

Sargent, William. *Crab Wars.* Hanover, N.H.: University Press of New England, 2002. A thorough history of the horseshoe crab, featuring conservation issues at Delaware Bay.

Sibley, David Allen. *The Sibley Guide to Bird Life and Behavior.* New York: Knopf, 2001. A great place to find out why birds behave as they do.

Stout, Gardner D., ed. *The Shorebirds of North America.* New York: Viking Press, 1967. For many years this oversized volume filled with gorgeous watercolor portraits by Robert Verity Clem was the bible on shorebirds. I found the discussion on market hunting especially helpful.

Weidensaul, Scott. *Living on the Wind: Across the Hemisphere with Migratory Birds.* New York: North Point Press, 1999. A wonderful study of bird migration.

ARTICLES, SCIENTIFIC PAPERS

Baker, Allan J. "The Plight of the Red Knot." *ROM Magazine*, Spring 2008, pp. 19–23. A fine overview of the knot's biology, migratory paths, and decline up to 2008.

Bauers, Sandy. "Geolocators Show Red Knots' Flights Extraordinary." *Philadelphia Inquirer*, August 11, 2010. A story about the results of data taken from the first few geolocators recovered from migrating red knots.

Gatowski, Meredith, ed. "Birding for Banded Shorebirds: The Basics—Updated!" *WHSRNews*, September 10, 2010. Also available at www.whsrn.org. A helpful primer on the dos, don'ts, and hows of bird banding.

Gill, Robert E., Jr., et al. "Extreme Endurance Flights by Landbirds Crossing the Pacific Ocean: Ecological Corridor Rather Than Barrier?" *Proceedings of the Royal Society*, vol. 276, pp. 447–57. Can migrating birds actually time their departures to take advantage of weather systems that provide tailwinds? Check out this article for the answer.

Moore, Robert. "Stemming the Tide: Shorebird Recovery in the 21st Century." *Birding*, vol. 41, no. 2, March 2009. An overview of the shorebird crisis in the western hemisphere.

Morrison, R.I.G., Allan J. Baker, Larry J. Niles, Patricia M. González, and R. Ken Ross. "Cosewic Assessment and Status Report on the Red Knot *Calidris canutus* in Canada." COSEWIC Secretariat, 2007. Available online at www.cosewic.gc.ca. A thorough, detailed study of the red knot's life history and conservation status.

Niles, Lawrence J., et al. "First Results Using Light Level Geolocators to Track Red Knots in the

Western Hemisphere Show Rapid and Long Intercontinental Flights and New Details of Migration Pathways." *Wader Study Group Bulletin*, vol. 117, no. 2, 2010. Here is a detailed report of the breakthroughs in tracking knot migration made possible through lightweight geolocators.

INTERNET AND MULTIMEDIA RESOURCES

The Cornell Lab of Ornithology. Want to hear what a red knot sounds like? Go to the Cornell Lab of Ornithology's Web site: www.allaboutbirds.org. Type "red knot" into the bird guide and then click "sound." Voilà! Many fascinating facts about *Calidris canutus* rufa are also provided.

Crash: A Tale of Two Species. This haunting 60-minute film, produced by Allison Argo, appeared on PBS's television series *Nature*. It is the story of the synchrony between the *rufa* red knot and the horseshoe crab at Delaware Bay, and of the sudden decline of both. Produced by Argo Films and Thirteen/WNET New York. Available on DVD.

"The Delaware Bay Blues." This song was written on the night of May 22, 2011, after the long day of banding described in Chapter Four. At dinner we started wondering what it would *feel* like to be a migrating red knot low on fuel, closing in on Delware Bay after days and nights of nonstop flight. A guitar appeared. Someone yelled, "I need eggs!" I wrote the rest and recorded it. Preview it as a downloadable CD at www.cdbaby.com and then type the title "The Delaware Bay Blues." Or, if you are using the song for conservation work, use the link http://dl.dropbox.com/u/23528178/The%20 Delaware%20Bay%20Blues_092211.mp3.

Friends of the Red Knot. This club was formed when a few students at the GreenMount School in Baltimore, Maryland, decided to get together and look for ways to help the red knot survive, especially around Delaware Bay. To learn more about the club's activities, go to www.friendsofthe redknot.org.

A Rube with a View (www.arubewithaview.com). To stay up to the minute on how the red knot is faring, and learn a whole lot more about its natural history, you can't beat this blog. Dr. Larry Niles, formerly the director of the New Jersey Endangered and Nongame Species Program, is on the front line of the struggle to conserve the *rufa* red knot. He and his wife, Dr. Amanda Dey, follow knots around the hemisphere, doing their best to document the crisis and to conserve the birds and horseshoe crabs. Larry's blog is entertaining, provoking, and wonderfully informative.

World Waders News Blog: A Global Pool for News on Shorebirds/Waders. At www.worldwaders .org/news.html. Here is a great way to keep up on news of shorebirds worldwide.

ACKNOWLEDGMENTS

Those who helped me with this book can be found all along B95's great hemispheric circuit. Many are biologists. We sometimes think of scientists as indoor people in white lab coats, but the scientists I met through this book are rugged, adventuresome, and equally at home indoors and out. They believe that discovery is found where the birds are. If that means journeying to remote places, even to the top or bottom of the world, hauling heavy equipment long distances, banding by flashlight at night, or struggling to prepare cannon nets in ferocious winds, so be it.

I thank Allan Baker and Patricia González for inviting me to Argentina and teaching me about banding, trapping, B95, and so much more. Allan patiently shared his knowledge of feather molt during a banding exercise, while Patricia taught me how to hold a shorebird correctly—and would not stand for anything less. I thank Luis Benegas for hosting me in Rio Grande, and for his great commitment to shorebirds. Graciela Alsina—"Gachi" to all—Mauricio Failla, and Cédrik Juillet all generously took the time to share their enthusiasm and to teach me. In Las Grutas, Silvana Sawicki and her daughter Luciana Ceccacci introduced me to the unique and inspiring Vuelo Latitud 40.

I thank Larry Niles and Amanda Dey for welcoming me to the yellow house at Reeds Beach, inviting me to join the banding crew, and answering my clouds of questions. In addition, Larry generously shared research materials from his book *Life Along the Delaware Bay*. His passion and energy for understanding and saving *rufa* is inspiring to me. I am grateful for the encouragement of Humphrey Sitters and Jeannine Parvin. Clive Minton, the genius who figured out how to catch uncatchable birds, has inspired and educated at least three generations of birders, and I am proud to be among them. I am grateful for the work and help of Mike Hudson, fifteen-year-old founder of Friends of the Red Knot. He is a total inspiration to me.

I also thank Smokey Swickla, Fred Layton, Jr., and Frank "Thumper" Eicherly, men who make their living from the water of Delaware Bay, for sharing their knowledge and perspective.

I thank Professor Theunis Piersma from the Netherlands, one of the world's great shorebird experts, for answering my questions by phone. He knows so much about red knots that a subspecies, *Calidris canutus piersmai*, was named for him.

I am grateful for the help and work of Jan van de Kam, a Dutch photographer who has traveled the globe for nearly forty years recording images of shorebirds. He has produced one of the world's great collections of nature photography. I thank him especially for taking beautiful close-up images of B95 and for sharing them.

I am grateful to Guy Morrison for flying the coast of South America with Ken Ross to find important shorebird sites and count birds, for continuing to count and study red knots, and for patiently answering my questions—which turned into a twenty-nine-page interview transcript.

At Mingan, Yves Aubry read and critiqued passages from the manuscript, and provided geographic information to help me create my description of B95's hypothetical flight between the Arctic tundra and Mingan. Yves patiently answered hundreds of my questions.

I thank the lysate expert Dr. Ron Berzofsky for sharing information and photographs about the bleeding of horseshoe crabs.

Brian Harrington, on whose work so much knowledge of *rufa* rests, granted me several long interviews. I thank Brian deeply for his many years of research, discovery, and exploration, and for writing so much of it down. Brian and his wife, Martha Sheldon, helped me find and select photographs from the work of the brilliant photographer David Twichell, who, along with the Manomet Center for Conservation Sciences, generously shared them for this project. I thank the staff of the Manomet Center, especially Martha Sheldon and Sue Chamberlain, for providing invaluable support and encouragement for this project.

My dear compadre Charles Duncan gave me the idea for this book by convincing me that it would be possible to document the plight of a magnificent bird through the story of a single individual—B95. His strong, creative support continues to this day. I salute Charles for having raised—with partners—nearly $2 million in an effort to try to keep *rufa* among the living.

Melanie Kroupa, my longtime friend and editor, was there for this book through every draft and every page. I can't thank her enough. And once again, I am grateful for the editorial help of Sharon McBride. I thank the skilled bookmakers at Farrar Straus Giroux Books for Young Readers, especially associate editor Beth Potter and senior designer Roberta Pressel, for their support, skill, and encouragement. I am grateful to my Nature Conservancy colleagues, especially Richard Jeo, Shannon Martin, and Mike Palmer, for support, encouragement, contacts in northern latitudes, and covering for me while I was writing this book. Thanks to Kristen Cappy of Curious City for supporting my work in so many ways.

Hannah Hoose and Ruby Hoose, my peerless daughters, often asked about this book and its hero and listened to my answers. May they grow old with *rufa* red knots in their lives. Sandi Ste.George, my wife, listened to me read chapter after chapter aloud, critiqued the work without bruising me, and gave me the pleasure of her company on trips to Argentina and other places along B95's highway. It is a joy to migrate through life with her.

Phil Hoose

PICTURE CREDITS

INDEX

Numbers in *italic* text indicate illustrations.